REVIVING OLD HOUSES

Over 500 Low-Cost Tips and Techniques

by Alan Dan Orme

A Garden Way Publishing Book

Storey Communications, Inc.
Schoolhouse Road
Pownal, Vermont 05261

Cover design by Cindy McFarland
Text design and production by Therese G. Lenz
Production assistant, Kelly Madden
Illustrations by Brigita Fuhrmann
Edited by Gwen W. Steege and Constance L. Oxley

Printed in the United States by Arcata Graphics
First Printing, June, 1989

Library of Congress Catalog-in-Publication Data
Orme, Alan Dan, 1933-
   Reviving old houses: over 500 low-cost tips and techniques/Alan Dan Orme.

   Includes index.
   ISBN 0-88266-563-4:
   1. Dwellings--Remodeling--Amateurs' manuals.   I. Title.
TH4816.O75 1989
643'.7--dc20

                   89-45220
                     CIP

CONTENTS

PREFACE

As I now complete this manuscript, I send it on to you, my reader, with a sense of joy in sharing with you the delight and satisfaction that a professional can find both in creating with one's hands and in beautifying something left by earlier generations.

I am especially thankful to my friends who have taught me many things I did not learn in my youth as a carpenter and who have encouraged me in the long evolution of this manuscript. I am especially grateful to Kevin Kelly, who, being an editor himself, was an encouragement to me in very practical ways. I am thankful to Ruth Wedel for her never-ending enthusiasm, from her first reading of the beginning chapter. I am most grateful to Lois Pitcher for her services as a proofreader when she was supposed to be a house guest. And I will never forget the advice and frequent help of Lee Moody and Brian Striggon, both of whom seem to know how to do anything that requires skill with the hands.

As a minister of the gospel, how can I forget to thank my Creator and Redeemer for making me, as He made all human beings, with the capacity to integrate profound thoughts and views about life and eternity with such a mundane subject as dwelling places and the unleashing of the creature's creativity in connection with them.

Finally, may I thank you, my reader, for your listening to some of my advice, which is given with the wish that a large measure of the happiness and fulfillment that I have found in making the renovation of an old house a part of my daily life and schedule may be yours also.

1
REVIVING YOUR OLD HOUSE

This book is about the romance of reviving old houses. It is written with the hope of passing on to you the thrill of participation in history, along with the wonderful satisfaction of owning a piece of history and, through renovation, giving it the unique stamp of your own personality and abilities. It is not a contractor's guide to renovation nor an architect's guide, but it is a manual of tips that I have learned from my own experience. I hope that my descriptions of what has worked for me will make it possible for you, the owner and budding craftsperson, to do a satisfactory job of renovating your own home.

You *can* do it, as thousands of others have been able to do it. You do not need to call in architects and building contractors, the federal government, and three foundations as if your intentions were to restore the Library of Congress. With today's resources and marvelously improved building materials, you can do a better job with your lack of experience than many tradespeople did just a few years back. In fact, you can probably do a passable job of renovation without this book, but reading it will save you countless hours of trouble, many dollars in building materials, and a considerable amount of embarrassment at having made an unforgivable mistake in the process of renovation.

Many of the tips in this book have grown out of my mistakes as a builder when I was a young man. Others have come out of my experiences—both successes and mistakes—in renovating my own home. Still others have grown out of observation and reports of many people's restoration and renovation projects far and wide. To some degree, skill as a builder is not just the ability to work with tools, but it is the accumulation of knowledge of what will work and what will not work in a specific situation. In short, I hope to give you some of the wisdom of my own experience.

Always I have given attention to cost. Those people who go about renovation as if they were going to restore the Chartres Cathedral usually are not troubled about the high cost of their methods. But I assume that my readers are very concerned about limiting high costs: For the average home renovator, costs have to be kept at a minimum. It is my hope that the reader will be able to afford an old house and find that, although its maintenance costs may be slightly higher than those of a brand-new, ubiquitous developer's house, the benefits will be well worth the strain on the budget.

In most human endeavors of any great moment, the task being contemplated often seems impossible to accomplish. Often, however, individuals who are pushed into a course of action or who have themselves impulsively rushed headlong into it, discover that they have resources of ingenuity and perseverance that they never dreamed of. It is my hope that you will find these hidden resources in yourself as you take on your own renovation project.

Can you really renovate your own house when you have no experience in building?

Numerous factors prompt an overwhelming "yes" to that question:

- Advances in building, plumbing, and electrical products that favor the do-it-yourselfer
- Relaxed building codes that allow the use of these easy-to-use building products
- Great new tools at lower prices to do a good job with less skill required
- More information available

How do you get the time necessary to renovate a house?

This is perhaps a more pertinent question than whether or not you have the *ability* to renovate. If you really want to do it, however, you can find the time to do so. Take heart in the fact that the existence of labor-saving, leisure-creating devices have given the average person more time for "doing-it-yourself" than ever before. Consider

- Simplifying your lifestyle
- Throwing the TV on the junk pile

- Making your house your recreation
- Scheduling a renovation vacation for the whole family
- Inviting friends and relatives to join you for a renovation week-end
- Taking a leave of absence from your job, if possible—you'll pay fewer taxes, travel, and entertain less, and have less stress

Can you really save by doing your own renovation?
- Over the cost of contracted renovation you may save as much as 70 percent. Over the cost of hiring day labor you may save as much as 40 to 50 percent.
- You save the dollar value of your time that would be spent dealing with employees.
- You may save 50 to 90 percent on materials, because you have the flexibility to plan, look, wait, and improvise.
- You can save by using second-hand materials, which are not cost-effective at high wages and which tradespeople often will not willingly use.
- When you pay workers you are paying them with pre-taxed dollars. If you cut back on your employment and do most of the work yourself, you pay no taxes on the value of the labor.

Hopefully, the answers to the above questions will result in a resounding "yes." You can do it! You can renovate your own house. It will yield
- Great savings
- Great personal satisfaction over and above that of merely *owning* an old house
- Family pride in the family home
- An example to your children of such values as thrift, hard work, responsibility, and respect for history
- Considerable financial equity in most cases, providing security should you have to relocate or liquify your assets
- An absolutely unique place in which to demonstrate both your skills and your philosophy about life

2
First Steps

Finding the Right House

You may be in the process of looking for a house to renovate at this time. Once you think you have found the house of your dreams, you need to give some serious and objective consideration to it, lest it become the house of your nightmares.

First, you should learn something about the various processes involved in buying and financing houses. Next, you need to know how to inspect a house. Finally, you must consider with cold objectivity your needs, including the time, both in years and in hours per month, available for renovating a house; your notions of the ideal neighborhoods in your area; the styles of houses you prefer; and the size house and number of rooms you need. If you follow the guidelines outlined in the next few chapters, you will save yourself the great anguish of buying a house beyond your means or capabilities or of buying a house that is a very poor candidate for renovation.

Searching for an old house takes time and patience. Some cardinal rules should help you avoid painful mistakes:
- Don't be hurried.
- Don't be intimidated into
    - Limiting your search
    - Forgetting your needs and expectations
    - Examining the house less than thoroughly
    - Meeting the seller's conditions
- Don't be blinded to your needs by "falling in love" with a house.
- Don't pay the asking price (or anywhere near it) without trying to get it drastically reduced.

Consider the Costs of Buying an Old House

Before you begin to skim the classifieds or contact a realtor you should consider
- The ideal, as well as the highest price you might be able to afford
- An estimated monthly budget for restoration projects

How to Estimate Monthly Mortgage Payments

For each $10,000 borrowed for 20 years:

Interest Rate	Monthly Payment*
7%	$ 77
8%	$ 84
9%	$ 90
10%	$ 96
11%	$ 103
12%	$ 110
13%	$ 117
14%	$ 124
15%	$ 132

*Approximate figures; method of compounding will cause some variation. Figure 1/10 of this for each additional $1,000 borrowed.

Due to the compounding of interest, the amount one eventually pays for a house is astounding. In the early years of a mortgage most of the payment goes toward the interest, and only halfway through the term of the mortgage does the payment begin to make a good dent in the principal. Several rules of thumb will help you make a rough estimate of how much your house will actually cost over the term of the mortgage.

Long-term Cost of Mortgage

Interest Rate	Length of Time	How Much You Will Pay
8%	20-year mortgage	twice the principal
15%	20-year mortgage	three times the principal
10%	30-year mortgage	three times the principal
15%	30-year mortgage	four and a half times the principal

Kinds of Mortgages

It pays to become informed about the various mortgages that banks offer. Shopping wisely for your mortgage can save you many dollars over the life of the mortgage.

Fixed-rate mortgage. The interest rate and the monthly payment remain the same over the time of the mortgage. If the interest rate charged is low in an inflating economy, a fixed-rate mortgage is a borrower's delight because the monthly payment gets progressively less in real money during the years of the mortgage.

Adjustable-rate mortgage. The interest rate wanders up and down according to the current inflation rates. In an uncertain economy, it is a banker's delight and cuts the bank's losses if there is a high inflation rate during the term of the mortgage. The saving feature for the borrower is that this mortgage usually has a cap on how many percentage points it can rise, as well as a provision that a certain number of years must pass before each new increase. Without these safeguards, it is potentially deadly for the homeowner.

Second (or third) mortgage. This mortgage is usually secured by the value of the property only after the first mortgage is paid off. A second mortgage is sometimes used to finance the down payment or even the closing costs. It is sometimes provided by companies other than banks, by individuals or relatives, or sometimes by the seller as an incentive to buy the house.

Other Costs Involved in Buying a House

In addition to the mortgage itself, a variety of other costs typically arise when you purchase a house.

Points. Sometimes points have to be paid to the lending institution. One point is 1 percent of the loan.

Loan application fee. This is sometimes, outrageously but decidedly, nonrefundable.

Closing costs. These are sometimes from 5 to 10 percent of the

total loan, and include such items as the costs of
- Checking the title
- Checking your credit
- Administering the loan

Earnest money. You pay earnest money to the seller when you contract to buy a property. It serves as a guarantee that will be awarded the seller should you withdraw from your agreement to purchase for any reasons other than those stipulated by the contract. It goes toward the down payment if your offer is accepted. Earnest money is usually held by a real estate company or a lawyer. An amount of 1 to 10 percent of the sale price might be acceptable. It is advantageous if this money is placed in an interest-bearing account, with the interest tied to the principal. If this is not possible, the earnest money should be as little as possible.

Escrow. Some banks may make you put money in escrow when you enter into extensive renovation. This is an account (usually at low interest) upon which you will draw for repairs as needed.

Property taxes. Taxes are usually divided up, with the former owner and the new owner each paying for his or her share of the year.

Other costs. You may be invited to buy out remaining fuel oil or time left on an existing homeowner's insurance policy. The latter may be to your benefit, as old houses are sometimes hard to insure.

Diplomacy and Commonsense as Bargaining Strategies
- Do not do anything to degrade the house to the owner.
- Do not make an unnecessary enemy out of the realtor.
- Do not rely too much on the realtor to protect your interests, for he or she represents the seller and is thus trying to get the highest sale price possible.
- Do not let anyone know that you have made up your mind to buy the house under any conditions until you have a contract in hand.
- Do not make up your mind that the house is yours until it *is* yours.

Cutting the Price

It is rare, particularly when dealing with older houses in need of renovation, that a seller expects to receive the asking price of the house. It is up to you, the buyer, to pay as little as will possibly be accepted. Here are some suggestions for your negotiating strategy:

- Exercise the most extreme politeness, even if you don't trust those you are dealing with.
- Gently but firmly mention the flaws you have found and how much they are apt to cost you to fix.
- Let it be known that you are looking at other houses as well as this one.
- Make an offer twice as low as you expect to pay; the seller will surely not accept your offer, but will make a counter offer.
- Ask the owner to include certain repairs as a part of the deal.
- Ask the owner to include in the deal certain items, such as
  - Furniture
  - Tools
  - Appliances
  - Dishes
  - Restoration materials
- Ask the owner to pay your closing costs or give you the time remaining on the insurance policy to reduce your start-up costs.
- Explore the idea of the seller's giving you a second mortgage at a lower rate than the bank is giving you the first mortgage; if the seller is planning on investing the profit from the sale, the interest you are willing to pay him or her may be more than bank or other investment interest will yield.

Watch out for sharpies who just want to make a lot of money on a house that is worth little.

To get you through the legal technicalities, hire a real estate lawyer at an hourly rate. You may find you actually save legal costs incurred in broker-handled closings. Make sure your lawyer protects your interests adequately.

Owner-Sold Houses

The great majority of houses that are sold are handled by realtors. Even when you see For-Sale-by-Owner signs, you must remember that many of these will eventually be sold by a real estate company. Owner-sold houses may be a great bargain for the buyer, particularly if, for one reason or another, the present owner has a pressing need to sell.

• The owner may be willing to sell for less because no commission will be taken from the profit by a realtor.
• Because many people will not buy owner-sold homes, you may find you have the negotiating advantage of a buyer's market.

Special Cautions for Owner-sold Homes

If you are taking out a mortgage, the bank will protect its own interest by requiring proof that the title to the property is free and clear. Nevertheless, make sure that your lawyer certifies the following points:

• There are no liens against the property. Liens are of varying sorts:
    • General claims against the property
    • Mechanics' liens for labor or materials
    • Surety bail bonds
    • Tax liens
• The deed or the contract does not stipulate easements (right of someone else to use your property) or restrictive covenants.
• Every condition of sale is written down and *everything* that is included is specified.
• You are dealing with the legal owner.

Included in a Contract
(even when not specified)

• The house and all of its parts
• Anything piped into the plumbing
• Anything wired into the electrical system
• Trees or shrubs that are planted in the ground

Gas space heaters, dishwashers, chandeliers, ceiling fans, mantels, self-storing storm windows, stained-glass windows, wall-to-wall carpets, therefore, are included. By all rights, because they are permanently installed, gas ranges and gas dryers should be included, but usually people think they should not be: be sure to clarify your understanding, in writing.

Kinds of Real Estate
Contracts on Houses for Sale

A seller has several options when he or she puts a house on the market. Each brings certain advantages and disadvantages.

Exclusive agency. The listed broker can sell the house, but if the owner sells it without the broker's help, the owner pays no commission.

Exclusive right to sell. One broker collects a portion of the commission no matter who actually sells it. Brokers may put more effort and advertising money into properties on which they hold an exclusive right to sell.

Multiple listing. Any licensed broker can sell it. The successful salesperson and the listing broker share the commission.

Open listing. Property is offered for sale and a commission is paid to any broker who sells it.

Net listing. Owner sets a price and the broker collects anything above that price that he or she can get from the buyer. Understandably, this is illegal in some places.

Understanding the vocabulary and processes attached to house buying and selling is a big step toward educating yourself about your project. You now have considered
- Your own financial resources
- Costs of renovating and mortgaging a property
- Kinds of mortgages available
- One-time costs incurred at the time of purchase of a property
- Techniques for getting the best price possible
- Advantages and disadvantages of purchasing an owner-sold house
- Special legal precautions
- Real estate terminology

With these facts in mind, you are prepared to take a hard look at the house you are hoping to buy.

Checking the House Out

This section is about shopping for an old house that is *your* house, a house that will respond to your dreams, your values, your lifestyle. Because it will be a house that you will put a lot of yourself into, it is imperative that you choose well. Use the items of this chapter as a checklist to be read before and after seeing the house you are considering. If you think bringing this book along might make you appear to be a novice, make a handwritten copy or a photocopy of the checklist on pages 34-37 to carry with you and note all the things on both the debit and credit side. A realtor will rarely mention the negative things to you, and he or she may not have even a ghost of an idea about the best of all the good points: the potential of this house for renovation. Such notetaking shows you to be a knowledgeable and careful prospective buyer and may actually strengthen your negotiating position if you find yourself in an adversarial relationship with a realtor or seller.

Later, you are going to make a list of the things to be repaired, restored, or remodeled, the number of months it might take you, and the dollars you will likely spend on each project. Ultimately, if you decide to buy the house, you will go through the list again and rate the things to be done in order of priority.

Why Inspect?

After your first guided tour though the house by the owner or realtor, your interest is peaked and you want to know everything possible about the house. You have two options: You may find it economical or convenient to hire a reputable home inspector — or even a knowledgeable friend — who will go over every inch of the house with you, discussing all of the pros and cons he or she notes; such an inspector may charge a flat or an hourly rate, which you should agree upon in advance. Alternatively, you can undertake such an inspection yourself, following the guidelines below. Even though you are not an expert and your estimates are fairly wide of the mark, they will surely supply a more accurate appraisal of the house than no consideration of them at all. The long-run benefits of such an inspection are real:

- The inspection will give you confidence in whether to go for the house or to forget it.
- If you turn up any architectural scandal but you still want to buy the house, you not only can estimate the probable cost of renovation, but you also may be able to negotiate hundreds or even thousands of dollars off the purchase price. One termite-eaten sill, one leaky sewer pipe, or one rotted-through porch floor may bring the price down by thousands.
- Consider that this likely will be the biggest investment you will ever make; you must go into it with as much knowledge as possible.

Some real estate brokers may discourage you from doing an inspection or appear to be inconvenienced by all of this. You are the one who is forking out the money, however, and a year from now you will be glad that you inspected thoroughly.

Equipping Yourself for the Inspection

Let's say you have walked through a number of houses and have finally found one that really stirs your hopes and imagination. It's time for a more serious look. For a thorough inspection you will find the following equipment valuable:

- Old clothes or coveralls

- A ladder
- A pair of binoculars or opera glasses
- A powerful flashlight
- A ball bearing or marble
- An ice pick or penknife
- A pad and a clipboard

The *old clothes* are for romping around in dirty places. This is no time to look pretty—save that for when you are trying to get a loan at the bank. This is serious detective work. You are searching for a diamond, albeit a diamond in the rough.

Carrying along a *ladder* is, admittedly, a lot of trouble but it is foolhardy to buy a house as you'd buy a pig in a poke. You will need a ladder to get into the attic space to look for leaks in the roof, to spot problem areas in the ceilings, to check the quality of the chimneys, and to unearth any critters who might be living up there.

The *binoculars* (not for looking at the neighbors, as you might have thought) are of inestimable value for inspecting roofs, gutters, flashings, chimneys, peaks, and dormers without risking your very life.

The *flashlight* is for looking in attics, basements, and other dark, scary places.

The *ball bearing* or *marble* is for testing the level of floors. You don't necessarily expect that everything will be level in an old house, but it certainly is interesting and revealing to know which way things slope. And I wouldn't give you a nickel for a renovator who doesn't know which way his or her floors slope!

The purpose of the *ice pick* or *penknife* is for poking at things to see if they are rotten or termite damaged.

Inspecting Underneath the House

Begin your inspection by looking under the house. If it is built low to the ground with no basement, you may have to peer under it with the help of your flashlight and try to examine the following in ways short of crawling under the house on hands and knees like a common alley cat.

Look at the *sills* (the part of the structure that rests on the masonry foundation), the main *supporting beams*, and the *posts* that hold them up. You are looking for soundness, absence of rot, and termites. You also hope to ascertain that there are not *foundational elements* missing. Use the ice pick to test the soundness of the

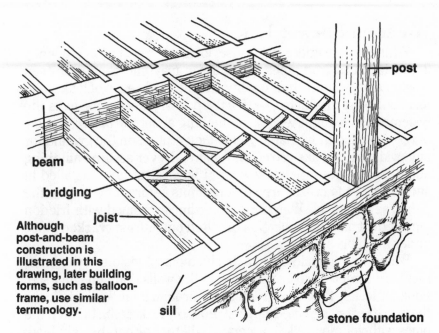

beam

bridging

joist

Although post-and-beam construction is illustrated in this drawing, later building forms, such as balloon-frame, use similar terminology.

post

sill

stone foundation

wood. On sills or large beams, the sapwood (the outer layer beneath the bark that was the younger, softer portion of the tree before it was cut) will often be dry and crumbly, but your pick should go no further than one-half inch before hitting something solid. If you find a soft spot in the wood, dig the surface away with your ice pick. Long hollow places going with the grain of the wood are evidence of termites, as are mud tunnels going up the masonry surfaces from the ground to the wood. These tunnels look rather like dried vines at first glance, but they are the termites' link with the earth, which most species of termites must have in order to stay alive. In some areas of North America, professional termite inspection is required before mortgages are granted or insurance policies are issued on a property.

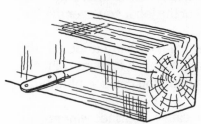

The outer portion (or sapwood) of old beams is often dry and crumbly, but on a sound beam, a probe should hit hard wood about 1/2 inch beneath the surface.

Carpenter ants are another fairly common insect pest. While they don't usually *cause* damage, they are attracted to wet, rotten wood. If you find carpenter ants, look for leaky roofs and pipes that might be soaking the framing.

Water and Sewer Lines

While you are under the house, look at the *sewer lines* (usually 3- to 4-inch cast-iron pipes, though you may find copper or even plastic) and evaluate their quality, neatness, absence of leaks, and location. Note in which *direction* the primary sewer pipe exits the basement; this might tell you something about the *distance to the sewer main* and thus enable you to look around on the ground for any evidence of leaks or recent repairs. Never assume anything about sewer lines or even sewers. I have seen them installed in such a way as to cross three different lots before they go into the public sewer main. Watch for sewer lines wrapped with friction tape or duct tape, an indication of rotted-out or frost-cracked pipes under the tape.

Water lines (usually 1/2- to 3/4-inch pipes) visible in the basement are a good measure of those in the walls that you can't see. Look for leaks. Powdery green stains around joints indicate leaks that were never corrected and will probably leak again. Scratch the pipes with your ice pick to ascertain whether or not they are lead: Lead is so soft that the pick will sink into it as if into wood, whereas the pick will scratch metallically against cast iron. Lead pipes must be replaced, as they are known to cause lead poisoning, cancer, and sterility. The experts are now even sounding the alarm about old copper pipes that were soldered with lead. If there are old copper lines, consider the complexity of the job if you ever decide to replace them.

Look carefully at the *bottom of the first floor* from underneath. Along with evidence of termite infestation, check for signs of leakage or rot, especially around places where you can see plumbing fixtures overhead.

Watch for *moisture* and its apparent cause—surface water from outside or plumbing problems. Is it run-through water that could be stopped by a drainpipe along the outside of the foundation? Could it be run-off from faulty downspouts or from the absence of both gutters and downspouts on the house? Very frequently this is the case. On the other hand, its location could indicate leaking sewer or water pipes.

To solve problems in wet basements requires an engineering triumph, but they can surely be solved, and some of the solutions are very simple (see pages 121-26). Generally you can assume that where there is a big water problem under a house, originally there was not this much water, and that some correctable drainage problem exists. The surest cure is to dig a trench around the entire foundation and lay in plastic drainpipe. This can be expensive if you don't do it yourself by hand and it can be difficult if your property is quite close to neighbors (see pages 124-26).

Electrical System

Look at the *wiring* that is visible from under the house. What *type* is it? If you find a knob-and-tube or other cloth-sheathed, non-grounded system, you know the wiring is old. Even many flexible conduit systems used insulation that gets crumbly with age. Open a junction box or two and look for overcrowding and particularly

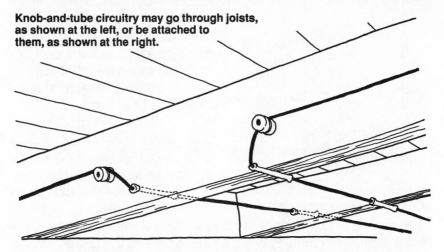

Knob-and-tube circuitry may go through joists, as shown at the left, or be attached to them, as shown at the right.

for crumbling insulation. Examine the overall condition of the wiring. Are there many places where new lines have been tied into the old wires with friction tape splices? Are the *splices* that you can see carefully done? What is the quality of any obvious *additions* to the system? Is it careless, crooked, and ragged, or a basically neat job? A lot of demerits earned on these questions will mean that you will need to make a major investment in wiring soon after you buy this house.

Hot Water Heater

Check out the *hot water heater* if it is in the basement. If you don't find it down here, it could be squirreled away in a closet, under a staircase, or standing hideously in a corner of the kitchen or bathroom. Hopefully, there is one someplace; never take such a fact for granted, however. Wherever you catch up with it, look it

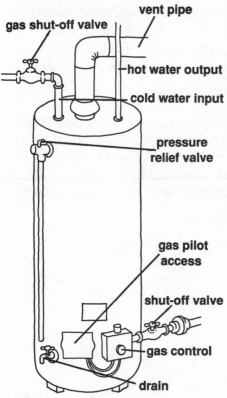

gas shut-off valve

vent pipe

hot water output

cold water input

pressure
relief valve

gas pilot
access

shut-off valve

gas control

drain

Gas hot-water heater.

over for an estimation of its *age*. Sometimes the connecting pipes and the fittings, where they have been screwed onto the heater, will give you a better clue than the enameled cover of the heater itself (which is *only* a cover, not the tank itself). Heaters that are as old as Methuselah, sometimes have nice clean enamel covers on them. Feel around the bottom for evidence of *drip* or *rust*, which usually means that the tank itself has succumbed to old age and is rusting away. Note the capacity of the heater. A 30-gallon natural gas heater will recover only about 27 gallons per hour.

Is this heater gas or electric? In spite of the fact that in most areas of North America electric heaters are a more expensive way to heat water, many people prefer electric. Should you decide to change over to a gas-fueled water heater, you will have to install a chimney or vent pipe to take off the fumes. If your house currently has an electric heater, it may be that the former owners installed it because they were unwilling and/or unable to install a vent and to run a gas line over to the location of the heater.

All gas heaters and most electric heaters have a setting so you can choose how hot to make the water. On electric heaters the

---

If an electric hot water heater fails to heat and the electric circuits are not broken, look for a reset button on the front of the heater or behind a metal shield. If a gas heater fails to heat, check to be sure the pilot is lit.

---

setting is often under the shield where you can't see it readily. If the heater is too small for your needs, you can increase the setting in order to make the same amount of water go further. Do not set it higher than 160° F. or it might scald someone, particularly if you have young children or elderly people in the house.

Heating System

Examine the *heating system* if it originates in the basement. Various heating systems are now in use, most commonly wood, coal, oil, or natural gas used in a steam, hot water, or hot air system. Make a note of the furnace *type* and *condition* as well as the location and state of deterioration of the *heat supply lines*. You may be an antique collector of considerable dedication—most old house buyers are—but you can surely do without an antique furnace. You may discover an old coal furnace converted to gas or oil. If it does not look all rusted out, it may be acceptable, though in most cases these old conversions are inefficient.

Inspecting the Interior of the House

It's time now to move to the interior of the house. Here, you will again examine the wiring and plumbing, in addition to general spaces and the condition of walls, floors, and trim.

Plumbing

You have seen the plumbing from the underside. Now consider whether *bathrooms* and *sinks* are located in approximately the right places or whether you are going to have to move everything. The old-timers sometimes put bathrooms in some unlikely places. As often as not they put them on a porch, sometimes without even taking the slope out of the floor before they installed the fixtures. These porches were sometimes half rotten before they were converted and poorly insulated after they were done over. Another common technique was to build an addition on the back of the house or a little privy-shaped box on the side of the main structure.

Do *pipes that supply the upstairs* run right up the surface of the walls or is it a sensible and tasteful installation? Check out all the *taps* and see how fast the water runs and whether rust runs out. Check also to be sure the hot water taps are operable. A lot of *rust* probably indicates really rusty pipes or a problem at the source of supply. Rust in the hot water only often means a dirty or badly deteriorated hot water heater.

Low pressure might mean a poor situation on the city water system or pipes almost filled up with mineral deposits. (I've seen them so clogged up that just a trickle comes out of a fully opened tap.) Look underneath sinks to see whether the drain pipes show signs of leakage, indicated by greenish, or sometimes white, crystals around the joints.

Bathrooms

Consider whether you could improve the existing bathroom(s) or whether major remodeling must be done. If the floors are of ceramic tile, observe whether the tiles are tight, loose, or missing altogether. If the floors are badly deteriorated, the holes may have to be filled and the tile covered with vinyl flooring. Small areas of damage may be patched with concrete or, better, repaired with tiles from another bathroom floor that is beyond salvation. Inspect ceramic bathtubs, sinks, and toilets for cracks and breaks. If the toilet rocks, it should be re-set. Evaluate the porcelain finish on cast-iron bathtubs and sinks.

Heating System

If the house has *radiators*, note their location. Check them for *leaks*, especially at the valves. Turn the valves on and off to see if they work. Sometimes radiators are missing. Although the original number may have been more than needed, you will certainly need at least one radiator in every room, except perhaps in the room directly over the furnace. You will have to go by guess on many of these things if it is summer. If the owner is present, be sure to ask about efficiency of the system, or, better still, ask if you can see heating bills from the previous winter. If they are no longer available, the utility company may be able to supply copies.

Kitchen

Notice the location and size of the *kitchen*. Are they both acceptable, or will you use its diminutive size and inconvenient layout as an excuse for serving an exclusive diet of TV dinners and frozen pizza four nights a week? Is there space in the kitchen (or elsewhere) for a *laundry area*? I don't know about you, but my idea of an old, renovated house does not preclude the basic conveniences that our advanced civilization has given us.

Living Areas

Is there a space for the kind of *parlor* or *formal living room* you would like? If you contemplate a *library* or *music room* are there spaces for them? Where would you put the TV and the stereo? Are there *enough rooms* for bedrooms for your brood—and the contemplated size of it in ten years?

Don't buy an old house that is too small, because luxurious size is often one of the bargains you get in an old house. Perhaps you, like I, have never seen a house, smaller than a mansion, that was too big for you. Other people seem to feel guilty when they are not using all of their space all of the time. You'll just have to decide how you feel about things. But if you live in a part of the country where winters are long and cold, remember that you will have to heat all of that lovely space somehow, unless you install heat zones and can close off unused parts of the house and leave them unheated.

Does the *layout* of the house give *enough privacy* for your family's lifestyle? Another of the great luxuries of most old houses is that rooms are laid out in such a way that you can get away from each other's noise. If this is desirable to you, make sure that this house suits that need.

Electrical System

Continue your inspection of the different components to the *electrical system*. Is the house served by a circuit breaker or a fuse box? What is the total amperage? A 200-amp service is more than adequate for a large family in a large house, but many old houses have only a 60-amp service. If the service is this small, you will have to rewire. If a fuse box, how many fuses are there? If the house has *circuit breakers*, it may have been completely rewired recently, though not necessarily. Can you determine if the hidden wiring is modern cable or an old, knob-and-tube system? What you can see of it in the basement and attic where it passes into the walls of the house should help you to guess. The knob-and-tube or two-wire system is not necessarily bad unless it has been carelessly repaired or is deteriorating because of age. The wire sizes are usually too small for anything but lights, however, and there is no ground, so you should replace it, if possible.

Look for the *number and evident condition of electrical outlets* and *light fixtures* in each room. Are they in working order and do they look safe? Blinking lights may indicate loose switches or

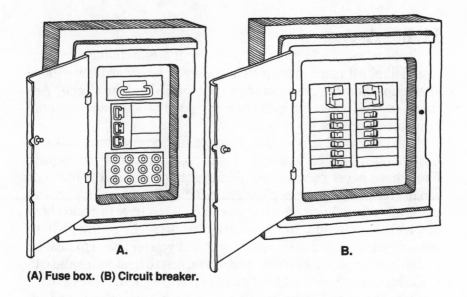

(A) Fuse box. (B) Circuit breaker.

outlets; these are dangerous and will need to be replaced as soon as possible.

If the house has a minimum number of electrical outlets as well as a minimum number of fuses, you will probably have to rebuild or extend the system, although sometimes one can balance the usage of the circuits. By avoiding placement of the refrigerator, color TV, microwave oven, toaster, and attic fan all on the same circuit and eliminating altogether very heavy users of electricity, such as electric heaters and air conditioners, you may be able to get along with the existing system reasonably well. If there are too few wall outlets, you will need to extend the system in order to avoid the use of extension cords, even if that means there will be too many outlets on one line. One can hardly imagine a more volatile electrical system than one largely made up of a mile of aging extension cords. For systems overextended with outlets, you simply will need continually to lecture your co-dwellers that just because there is an unused outlet on the wall doesn't necessarily mean that one can safely plug an electric popcorn maker into it, or a fuse will blow.

Ceilings

Take note of the *ceilings*. Give a light tap here and there. A hollow sound indicates that the plaster or the lath has pulled away from the joists underneath. Any sags in the ceiling should be investigated or mentally marked down as a mandatory need for a new ceiling. If you can lift the ceiling a half an inch or more with a broom handle, the ceiling obviously is loose. (When you push, do so very carefully or the whole shebang may come down on your head. I have seen one come down more or less in one piece, and to experience it is awesome!) Generally, ceilings, because of the force of gravity, aided and abetted by people jumping around on the second floor, and the absence of wallpaper, are likely to come apart and need replacement sooner than walls. Over the decades, wallpaper seems to preserve plaster better than mere paint does.

You probably ought to consider *marginally adequate ceilings* as candidates for recovering with gypsum wallboard (sometimes called plasterboard or drywall, or by the tradename Sheetrock). If the plaster has pulled away from the ceiling above it, however, because of its tremendous weight, it must all be torn off and the wallboard nailed against the lath. Be forewarned: It is a filthy job getting all that old plaster out of the house.

Many old houses have the distressing feature of *brick chimneys* on top of ceiling joists, with nothing but the ceiling to hold them up. Look for them especially over kitchens and bathrooms with no living space above them. There once was even a commercially prepared kit in which a stovepipe opening was bolted to the ceiling and to a saddle made of 4x4s upon which the bricks were then laid. When these chimneys were taken out of service, they were sometimes merely cut off at roof level and roofed over, leaving the main part of the chimney still in the attic. Because ceilings often contain

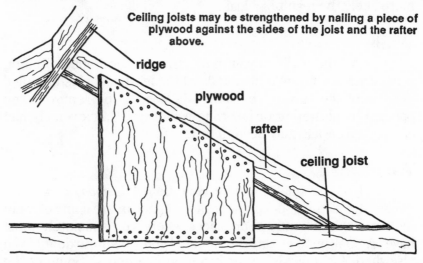

Ceiling joists may be strengthened by nailing a piece of plywood against the sides of the joist and the rafter above.

ridge

plywood

rafter

ceiling joist

minimal dimension joists, such piles of bricks frequently cause a whole ceiling, or part of it, to sag down five or six inches.

Sometimes the ceiling will retract a considerable distance when the bricks are removed. In other cases, the bricks must be removed, the ceiling jacked up, and a strengthening joist nailed alongside the sagging joist. Alternatively, one can tie the sagging joist to one of the roof rafters. To avoid placing all of the stress on

---

Rarely does plumbing ever repair itself. About the only exception is a small leak at the joint in an iron pipe just after you have replaced the joint. In this case a one-drip-a-minute leak, for example, will probably dry up in two days time.

---

one point of the rafter, nail a section of plywood against the sides of the rafter and joist (see illustration). Use a lot of 6d, preferably cement-coated nails and 1/2-inch plywood.

All stains on the ceiling plaster should be investigated for a source of leakage above. This is of utmost importance because it may be your only way of determining the condition of both the upstairs plumbing and the roof. If there are spots on the ceiling approximately under plumbing fixtures upstairs and no evidence of recent repair (new parts should be obvious), then you will probably experience the same leak under some or all conditions. The spots could be from an overflowed tub or stopped-up toilet, but are more likely the result of a leak.

Walls

Observe the *walls* as you move through the house. Rough, broken surfaces should be noted. At the least, any plaster pulled away from the lath on the walls will need to be removed and patched by plastering or inserting wallboard. In extremely bad cases, entire walls may need to be replaced.

Woodwork

Check out the quality and the condition of the *woodwork* in the house. Are all the doors present and original, or are some of them modern replacements? For places where you absolutely must have original, good quality doors, could you substitute doors from elsewhere for nonexistent or inappropriate doors? Some of the replacement doors may be old enough to complement the house; it is not uncommon to have one or two doors with horizontal panels (usually made after 1910) mixed in with the four-vertical-panel doors that were common in the last century and in the first decade of this century.

Windows and Doors

Watch for broken *windows* and *rotted window sash*. Sash is apt to rot at the bottom where the water settles as it runs off the glass, usually first at the joint between the bottom and the side piece of the sash. Gently test these areas with your faithful ice pick, and make a judgment on which you would need to replace. Look, too, for *replacement windows* that do not match the originals. It is most important for the front windows and other street-side windows to be original or authentically matched. Side and rear window replacements might be allowed to stay if they are in good shape and not monstrosities. The general, overall effect of a house is so often determined by its windows that they may be the most important architectural feature of the building. If you must replace "modern" windows to regain that beauty and integrity, it is well worth the investment.

Check the fit of both *windows* and *doors*. A common problem is doors that are badly warped or that have been fitted by one who was a wood butcher rather than a carpenter. In fact, it is rare to see an old house that has not yet been renovated or restored that doesn't have some nasty little scandal such as this. There are several ways to solve this problem: good weatherstripping, a storm window, thicker window or door stop, or even a piece of wood glued on the edge of the door or sash to fill up some of the empty space. Avoid nailing extension strips into doors, because nails tend to work loose and cause problems, and they make planing nearly impossible.

Floors

Are the *floors* good? Would a thorough cleaning and a fresh coat of shellac or polyurethane be all they need or must they be sanded? Or are they so bad as to require wall-to-wall carpeting? I have seen floors that looked like a plowed field due to moisture underneath. There may be little hope for such a floor except to carpet it or lay another floor. On the other hand, don't discount the rich beauty of a floor that seems hopelessly banged up. Once you have sanded and beautifully finished it, and then partially covered it with a braided or oriental rug, it will be transformed. This is especially true if your taste in antiques runs in the direction of primitives.

Generally speaking, no floor is too rough for sanding. It may take a tremendous amount of sanding to level it, however, especially if the boards are warped, as is often the case with oak floors. True, some floors are hopeless:

- A floor so warped that all the nails, tongues, and grooves that hold it together will be exposed when it is sanded level
- A floor with a long seam or joint running across the grain at a prominent part of the floor
- A floor patched with mismatched lumber that cannot be cured by staining or replacing the patches

As you examine the floors, watch for obvious *dips, sags, or slopes*. Your ball bearing should be of help here. When you find a slope, look along the baseboards at the floor line to see if there is a large crack showing a fairly recent settling. It may be as big as an inch or two. Floors will often slope toward a chimney, but the tell-tale crack should warn you of a recent problem. A room that shakes badly when you walk or jump on it may also have some problems underneath. Such settling, sloping, and shaking might be the result of a number of problems, either serious or inconsequential. Investigate and try to form an educated opinion about the causes.

Serious Problems
- Rotted sills, posts, or joists
- Termites making their dinner out of something underneath
- Someone's engineering mistake in a previous remodeling attempt
- Missing bridging (the criss-cross supports between the joists at the middle of the span; see page 15)

Inconsequential Problems
- Too much weight on the floor
- A settling that has not stabilized
- A not-serious weakness in the original design

Give special consideration to the *floors in the kitchen and bath-room*. Check for rot around the toilet and near the sink with your ice pick. One sometimes finds a toilet or bathtub that, were it not for the sewer pipe holding it up, would drop into the basement.

Decoration

Note any *absence of decoration* throughout the house such as moldings, paneling, and the like.

Fireplaces

If there are *fireplaces*, observe if they have been ruined by the loss of tiles or modernization of the mantel. If they have been cemented shut at the flue, it may be a blessing in disguise, both because old fireplaces are often unsafe and because they can suck heat out of your house almost as fast as your heating system will produce it. (For more detail, see pages 147-48.) If the fireplace opening itself has been covered over, tap on it to determine how difficult it might be to reopen it so that it could become beautiful again. It may have just a thin wall of bricks or wallboard covering it.

Looking in the Attic

The *attic* may be hard to get to, or you may have to look in through a ventilator or up through a small hole in the ceiling of some closet. You may suspect all sorts of creepy-crawlies up here, but, in fact, sealed-off attics are usually free of such things. In the summer, however, watch out for wasps! A careful sweep with your powerful flashlight will reveal a great deal.

Insulation

Is the house insulated? How deep is the insulation? Often the blown-in kind of insulation settles a great deal and you may be surprised at how little is left, even if the owner said it was seven inches thick. Don't worry a great deal about this, because this kind of insulation is very easy to add to. It is, however, just one more thing you'll have to do.

Asbestos insulation is now judged to be dangerous and government standards call for its removal. It is of particular concern if it is exposed to the heating system or has other means of getting into the air of the house. You may suspect that any old, fibrous insulation contains asbestos, but there is no way to be certain of its content without professional testing. It is a bargaining chip worth several thousands off the house because professional removal is quite expensive.

Unwanted Visitors

With your eyes and with your nose test for *evidences of wildlife*. You don't wish to buy an amusement park for squirrels or a bird sanctuary or a place for bats to hang out after a nighttime of fun. Pigeons will be known by the feathers and trash connected with their nests. Also, you will almost certainly see them roosting around on the outside as if they owned the place free and clear. Bats create a strong, dirty, musty odor. The first step in eliminating these nonpaying visitors to your house, if you should buy it, will be to put screening over vents and repair any holes in the roof, eaves, or walls that allow them access. Screening decreases the opening by about one-half, so be sure the vent is adequate for the space being ventilated. All of these critters believe in the validity of squatters' rights, and cannot be expected to go away without industrial-strength intimidation.

Wiring

Check out the *wiring* up there in the attic and compare it with the wiring in the rest of the house. Watch for damage by rodents. Squirrels are known to form a taste for old wire insulation when they get hungry enough. They are likely to eat only wires that are in plain view, so your main concern is to evaluate what is visible.

Roof

Most important, here is the place to find out about the *roof from the underside*. Make a mental note of any irregularities or peculiarities in the roof so you can see how they look from the outside later on. Looking through the cracks of the roof boards, can you see what the original roofing material was made of? If there are merely slats with wide spaces between, the roof was originally wood shingles, slate, or tile. Determine how many roofs have been nailed on top of the original roofing material, if possible.

Watch for *evidences of leaks in the roof*, especially where you saw stains in the ceiling below. You might see dark wood where a suspected leak has occurred, particularly right under a valley in the roof or near a chimney flashing, where most roof leaks occur.

Watch for rotted out roof boards or holes in the eaves, evidenced by light coming through where the slope of the roof begins. These are places that will have to be repaired immediately.

Look at the *chimneys* as they go through the attic, noting their location and condition. Watch for *unused chimneys* as described on pages 23-24. One of these could explain that horrendous sag in the kitchen ceiling that you were worried about earlier.

A Walk around the Exterior

How is the *siding and exterior wood*? Are there any bad areas that will likely need replacing? Look for any vertical area of the siding where the *paint is peeling off*, it is usually a dead giveaway that there is water seeping in behind the wall, either from a leaky or backed-up gutter or even from a leaky roof. Poke any place that looks rotten with your ice pick. Paint will never stick to rotten wood for very long.

Watch for *leaks in the eaves* (the roof overhang), manifested by missing or rotted boards or peeling paint.

Check all *window sills* within reach to see if they are rotted. Test for softness with your ice pick if they look rotten. If they are for the most part badly worn, you will need to go back in and check out the ones you can't reach from the outside by opening the windows from inside.

Around the eaves or near ventilators look for *feathers or bird droppings*, which indicate the existence of avian doorways into your attic.

Watch for any *missing or deteriorated original decoration*. Take note of the difficulty or ease of replacing this decoration. Sometimes it is missing because it rotted and fell off. In other cases, the house was the injured party in a criminal scheme of *remodeling* that *remuddled* the hereditary beauty of the house.

Masonry

If this house has a masonry exterior you will be looking for other sorts of things in your examination. If the window casing and sills are wood rather than masonry, check there for deteriorated wood, as well as checking all other exposed wood, such as eaves and cornices, as described above. Owners of stucco, brick, or stone houses often tend to forget that these parts must be painted and otherwise maintained as with an all-wood exterior. Your main concern, however, is to assess the condition of the masonry walls.

Usually brick or stone houses will have a *crack* or two running from bottom to top. It is caused by an ever-so-slight amount of settling at one point or another that can be filled with caulk and forgotten. Watch out, however, for evidence, such as large cracks, bowed walls, or many fallen bricks, that a whole wall or section of the house is falling into the street. If it is, it is usually because a foundation is settling for one reason or another. This exact situation has caused the Tower of Pisa to lean, and various bright ideas as to how to correct the problem have only made it lean farther. This could happen to you, and while Pisa's leaning tower has become a tourist attraction, yours is likely to attract only the building inspector.

Watch for *rotted mortar* between the bricks or stones. Test with your ice pick at numerous places. If it is bad all over, you are in for a long project of tuck-pointing the mortar if you buy this house. Bricks themselves can be damaged by moisture or freezing, especially if they have stayed wet, if ivy has been grown on the building, or if the bricks were no good in the first place. Small areas of decay can be plastered or painted over if they are first wired or covered with lath.

If the house is constructed of stucco over wood lath, look for the dark spots that indicate that the *lath is rotted under the stucco*. Take note of how much stucco needs to be replastered.

Porches

Porches are usually the worst disaster on the exterior of an old house. You may find them in an advanced stage of gangrene or already amputated. Worst of all is when they have suffered reconstructive surgery at the hands of a mechanic who had no taste in old houses, for the remodeling of porches has probably destroyed more homes than termites have. I could wax eloquent about the perfectly beautiful homes I know of that have been destroyed by rooms built on porches. Whenever I see such a house, I think of an exceedingly beautiful maiden who is wearing wretched, ill-fitting clothes. In the case of the maiden, the solution is simple. In the case of houses, the solution is complex because the damage is permanent. These old porches were often very large and are indeed expensive to rebuild. To the buyer's benefit, however, it is not unlikely that on some houses, the *absence* of an original porch in mint condition could devalue the house quite substantially. The only qualification is that you be able to see the potential in the building as it stands. With your savings, you may be able to pay for not only a new porch, but also a garage, a fence, and several other items.

If the house still has more or less original porches, check out the *railings*, *balusters*, and *porch posts* for rot by poking your ice pick at the bottom where the water settles. There are remedies for any problems you turn up (see pages 97-103), but it is good to know what you are up against.

If there originally was *gingerbread* (ornate, sawn-wood decoration such as brackets, posts, and finials), is it present and in reparable condition? If not, could it be duplicated with the original or a similar pattern?

Watch for peeling paint on the porch ceiling as a sign of a *leaky roof*. If the ceiling has been recently painted, the sign of leaks will be dirty spots where the water dripped through.

Test the floor for sturdiness by jumping a little on it. (Not too hard though: you wouldn't want to go through.) Look at the floor boards. If they are in good shape, you are probably looking at one well-kept house, because porches are mighty hard to keep in top condition.

Stand back and view the house with its porch in mind.

- Was this the *profile* of the original porch or does it look like something out of a mail-order catalog stuck on an empty wall?
- Are the posts too long or (more often) too short?
- Is the porch too wide?
- Should the porch be wider than the house itself with wrap-around ends?
- Are posts placed in a pattern that obscures the windows?

The Roof and Its Parts

While you are off at a vantage point looking at the lower parts of the house, begin your evaluation of the roof and related matters. Now is the time to use those binoculars.

Look carefully at the condition of the *roof shingles*. Watch for torn shingles, patches, or unevenness due to curled shingles and missing pieces.

As mentioned on page 28, it would be helpful to know how many *layers of roofing* are on the house. If there are three or four, then you are due for a fresh start the next time you need to put on a roof. Roofing builds up tremendous weight and, furthermore, the top-

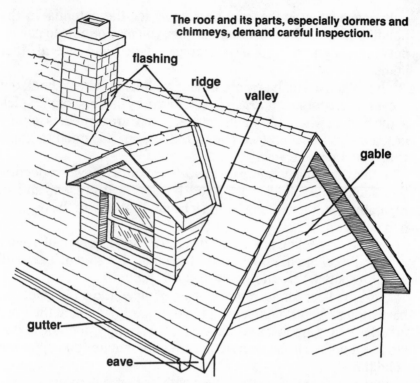

The roof and its parts, especially dormers and chimneys, demand careful inspection.

flashing

ridge

valley

gable

gutter

eave

most layers of an overloaded roof don't stay nailed very well. The number of layers of roofing that a roof can withstand is determined by the pitch of the roof and the kind of rafters and roofing materials. Large diamond-shaped shingles, for example, are much lighter than the common 3-tab, horizontal shingles.

Are *roofs on porches and additions* in good condition?

Check the *flashing* (sheet-metal protection) around the chimney and at places, such as dormers, where a vertical wall adjoins the roof. Check the condition of *roof valleys* (places where two different pitches of the roof adjoin).

Look at the *gutters* and *downspouts* to check for deterioration. Give special attention to *built-in gutters*, which can be real owner-breakers. If the roof needs replacing, you might consider at the same time covering these with plywood, re-roofing the whole roof, and then attaching metal gutters to the edge of the roof.

Look for *sags on the surface of the roof* that might mean a broken rafter or some rotted out boards under the roofing, occasionally caused by a leak that has been allowed to exist for many years.

Look for *sags and dips in the ridge of the roof* (the horizontal line formed where one side of the roof meets the other side). There has to be an explanation, either old or new, for an irregular roofline, and you need to make some guesses about the cause and then try to confirm them. The sag in the middle or dip on one end might represent

• Weakened foundations
• Termites in the walls
• Rotted places in the walls
• Exterior walls that have bowed out in the area directly under the sag

If you can determine that whatever caused the sag has been corrected or halted and that an on-going process of deterioration does not exist, you can simply enjoy the picturesque beauty of an old house with a sag in the roof. *Settling* of a house might be a natural part of the building process. In some areas, for example, frame houses were built on piers that were merely bricks laid directly on the ground. The foundations usually settled by the time the windows and trim of the house were installed. Then, instead of lining windows and doors up with the floors, they were installed in plumb and level.

A *sag in the eave line* might indicate a broken (or rotted) eave. If *both the ridge and the eave sag down* on one end, you might suspect

• Settling in the foundation
• Termite damage in the wall directly below the sag
• Improper foundation and settling at the weak place
• A very heavy chimney that might have not had a sufficient foundation for its weight, and thus pulled the part of the house to which it is attached down with it over the years
• Some sort of drainage problem that keeps the ground continually drenched under the foundation

Stand Back and Look

While you are on the outside, take a few moments to look at this house and imagine its potential. Is it really *your* house? Is it beautiful in outline and details? Are the windows the right shape for this style of house? What would be the effect of shutters, a front door more in keeping with the style of the house, or the replacement of the ugly, aluminum storm door that some practical soul installed? Is the silhouette of the original house and its additions a nice one or does it look like an unplanned collection of rabbit warrens? If chimneys, porches, shutters, or decoration are missing, can you imagine how the house would look after these essential ingredients are replaced? Would it be necessary to replace them in order to have the house look right? Consider how the house might be improved in its look. What if it were given a multicolor paint job to highlight its gingerbread?

Your inspection of the house has given you hard information about

- The underside of the house, including sills, beams, posts, sewer and water lines, possible drainage problems, wiring, hot water heater, heating system
- The interior of the house, including bathroom and kitchen plumbing; radiators; location and size of kitchen; overall space and layout; electrical system; ceilings; walls; woodwork, windows, and doors; floors, especially in kitchen and bathrooms; fireplaces
- The attic, including insulation, possible animal life, wiring, roof underside
- The exterior of the house, including siding; eaves, missing decoration; if masonry, cracks, leans, rotted mortar; railings, balusters, trim, floors, ceilings, and overall design of porches
- The main and porch roofs and their parts, including roofing materials, flashing, gutters, sags and dips in both the ridge and eaves of the roof

With this objective information in hand, it is now time to mull over your decision.

Inspection Checklist

Make a photocopy of this checklist to take along for your inspection tour. Use the "notes" column to remind yourself of materials, styles, or special features or problems of points under consideration.

	Very Poor	Poor	Acceptable	Good	Excellent	Notes
Basement:						
Masonry foundation						
Sills						
Beams						
Supporting posts						

	Very Poor	Poor	Acceptable	Good	Excellent	Notes
Joists						
Underfloors (sub-flooring)						
Furnace						
Heating pipes						
Water lines						
Sewer lines						
Electrical wiring						
Hot water heater						
Moisture						
Living Areas:						
Plumbing						
Water pressure						
Heating system						
Number of rooms						
Layout of rooms						
Fuse or circuit breaker box						
Electrical outlets						
Switches						
Light fixtures						
Ceilings						
Walls						
Doors						
Windows						
Floors						
Kitchen floor						

	Very Poor	Poor	Acceptable	Good	Excellent	Notes
Bathroom floor(s)						
Attic:						
"Critters"						
Electrical wiring						
Insulation						
Ventilation						
Chimneys						
Roof underside						
Roof:						
General condition						
Valleys						
Flashing						
Gutters						
Ridge line						
Eave line						
Dormers						
Chimneys						
Exterior:						
Siding						
Masonry						
Windows						
Window sills						
Settling						
Decoration						
Porches:						
Design						
Decoration						
Posts						
Balusters						
Steps						
Floor						

	Very Poor	Poor	Acceptable	Good	Excellent	Notes
Under-structure						
Roof						
Profile:						
Design						
Additions						
Porches						
Missing parts						
Location on lot						
Landscaping						

Mulling it Over

You have done a thorough inspection of the house that you propose to restore. It is now your task to make a decision based first upon the data you have observed and collected. Use the following checklists to guide your objective evaluation of the property. Score each item on a scale of 1 to 5, from poor to excellent. Then calculate the average score for each section. After all these points have been considered to your satisfaction, you can allow yourself to pay attention to your less pragmatic, emotional reactions to the house.

Does the size and layout of the house suit your needs now and in the foreseeable future?

Unless you can somehow come to terms with your need for space by readjusting your priorities or reassigning space, then you will do poorly to buy this house if it does not score high on this list.

	Location	Size	Notes
Living room	_____	_____	_____
Dining room	_____	_____	_____
Kitchen	_____	_____	_____
Bathrooms	_____	_____	_____
Bedrooms	_____	_____	_____
Library	_____	_____	_____

	Location	Size	Notes
Study			
TV/music room			
Recreation room			
Workshop			
Storage area			
Garden			
Outdoor recreation			

Possible ways to gain more space
- *Addition* to building
- *Division* of existing space
- *Lofts* in high-ceilinged rooms
- Development of *attic* or *basement*
- Adding *additional building* for shop or storage

Is the location of this house one that you can live with?

This checklist is serious business. Unless you and your family are going to be comfortable in this location you should be looking for another house. No bargain, no amount of beauty, can overshadow the fact that a house is located where you definitely do not want to live.

	Location	Notes
Near creeping slums		
Near expanding business district		
Traffic congestion		
Close neighbors		
Quality of schools		
Distance to work		
Distance of shopping areas		

Factors to consider in estimating the growth or deterioration of the neighborhood:
- Number of restorable houses in the neighborhood
- Climate of restoration in the particular city
- Zoning (can the buildings be used as single- or multi-family residences? for business?)

- Zoning of surrounding area
- Number of houses renovated or in the process of renovation
- Average cost of old houses (Too high for private homes? Dirt cheap so that slum lords are apt to take over?)
- Encroachment of slums, subdivided rental property, and business in recent years

What did your thorough inspection of the house turn up?

It would be well to go through your notes and make a list of all the serious negatives that are going to take a considerable amount of time and money to correct.

Next, make three lists, as described below, with a note by each item estimating the probable time and money involved:
- Major projects needed to be done before your family can move in
- Major projects required to keep the building from rapid deterioration
- Major projects required before you will consider this a comfortable and livable house

Will your budget be able to handle the proposed renovation?

To determine this important factor, begin by listing your *assets*:
- Amount of cash available in a comfortable situation
- Amount of cash available in a worst-case situation
- Amount of cash available in a drastic search for funds

Revise your monthly budget to project what you will need if you buy this house. Include
- Renovation expenses
- Mortgage payments
- Taxes
- Insurance

List all the funds you could funnel into renovation by cutting back on other activities. Might you be willing and able, for instance, to cut back on funds spent on vacations, periodicals, movies and parties, eating out, or new clothes?

Replotting Your Time and Budget

If things do not effortlessly fall together, this does not mean that you cannot afford or manage the house. If you're short of *cash* for

renovation you might
- Ask the seller for a second mortgage
- Convince the bank to *reduce the down payment* required
- Plan on using more *secondhand materials,* which require more labor and less cash
- Take out a *short-term loan* or *sell something*
- *Readjust priorities* to put off expensive projects

If you're short of *time* for projected renovation you might
- *Readjust* your schedule
- Plan to *hire help* just for the start-up crisis
- *Call on friends* to help

You should now have in hand some very concrete data upon which to base your decision about whether or not to buy this house you have examined. You can consider the facts and figures of
- Space and layout of the house
- The location of the house
- The nature of the neighborhood
- The extent of renovation required
- The adequacy of your budget and your time to deal with the renovation

3

ORGANIZING FOR WORK

Planning Ahead

The decision-making, mortgage-shopping, and papers-signing are now behind you. You are eager to put right all of the problems in your wonderful old house, transforming it into the house of your imagination. How to begin? Successful house renovation requires that you *plan ahead*, lest in a few months you be like the man who jumped on his horse and ran off in all directions—and lest your house look like the house that Jack built when you get through.

Nothing is so sad to the house renovator as to discover, "I didn't think it would look like *that* when I started this improvement." This realization is often followed by the equally sad experience of tearing out last year's restoration only one year later because you did not think ahead. Proper planning will save you many renovator's headaches, and good lists will
- Keep you doing first things first
- Enable you to make the best use of your time and money
- Permit you to garner free or cheap materials for upcoming projects

Making a List of Priorities

You have made a list of things that need to be done on this house. Now is the time to organize your data into lists of priorities, with lots of white space for adding things and making explanatory notes. Next to each item on your lists make a note of the probable expenditure of time and money required. Note also what materials will be needed for each project; for long-term projects you will often be able to collect materials well in advance of work on the project, allowing you to search out sales or secondhand materials.

- **List 1:** Those projects that need immediate attention because cosmetic or structural degeneration is ongoing, delay will radically escalate costs, or family safety and health are at risk
- **List 2:** Those projects necessary for adequate livability, judged by aesthetic, emotional, and practical criteria
- **List 3:** Those projects you would like to do in the foreseeable future
- **List 4:** Those projects that you know will be nice—or necessary—to do eventually
- **List 5:** Fun projects, to be saved for their recreational and encouragement value; like garnishes to a good meal, they should be interspersed with the more serious fare

A word of caution. Many renovators, especially new homeowners, become overwhelmed by the tasks they have overtaken and "burn out" before their dreams are realized. To avoid this problem

- Don't do too many fun things while avoiding the imperative projects in List 1, thus playing your way into inevitable disaster.
- Don't open up too many cans of worms at one time; finish as much as you can before starting something else.
- Don't embark on projects you haven't enough time or money to finish in the time allotted.
- Seek the encouragement of other house renovators.

Pictures and Drawings

Before you replace a single board or drive a solitary nail, take pictures of the house, including shots of the ugliest features of the building. These will form the basis of a pictorial history of the renovation of your house that will be a wonderful memento, a historical resource, and personal encouragement as you see how far you have come.

As important as these photos will be "for the record," they serve a very practical purpose as well. Take straightforward shots of each side and of each detail, such as an ornate peak, a small porch, or a bay window, and use these to make working drawings ("blueprints") of your house. Specifically, you will need drawings of

- *Elevations* (a flat view with no perspective) of each side (scale: 1/4" = 1')
- *Details* of smaller features that will need restoration or change

(scale: 1" = 1' or larger)
- *Floor plans* (outlines of the floor(s) of the house), including all windows and doors, stairways, fireplaces, plumbing fixtures (scale 1/4" = 1')

These drawings might be assigned to your teenager or a friend who has just taken a drafting course. But even without experience you can make drawings adequate for your purposes. Once drawings are made, make several photocopies of the originals, and experiment only on the copies, retaining the masters for your files.

- Draw in pencil (to facilitate erasure).
- Collect as many dimensions as possible on a rough drawing.
- Use dimensions you *know* to estimate dimensions you *can't reach* by measuring the distance on the photos. Such dimensions might include the width of a siding board or window casing. Note these visual measuring marks right on the drawing.
- For floor plans, indicate the total size of windows and doors, including surrounding trim; estimate 6 inches for wall thickness; make one plan for each floor.
- Draw every contemplated change on a photocopy before proceeding; don't add even a shutter unless you try it out first on a copy.
- Make a set that "grows" with the house, revised only after the actual change is made.

Alternative, Penny-Pincher Solutions to Common Problems

Many of the most common problems in old houses are rather superficial and can be solved temporarily, or even permanently in some cases, by cosmetic tricks that are both quick and inexpensive. Here are a few suggestions.

Quick Tricks for Common Problems

Problem	Penny-Pincher solution
Bad walls	Cover with rugs and tapestries
	Apply wallpaper, which not only covers a lot, but even strengthens the plaster

Problem	Penny-Pincher solution
	"skin" (large cracks and holes should be filled with joint compound and lightly sanded before paper is applied)
Modernized bathroom	Use primitive furniture or old dresser mirror(s)
	Use old lamps or lighting fixtures
Too small door or window	Install shutters to enlarge the opening visually
	For window, install a window box
Plywood flush door	Apply wood panels or moldings in a pattern similar to other doors in the house
Screened-in porch	With decorative wood trim, outline on the exterior any gingerbread, moldings, or balustrades that have been covered by screening
Plain, bare rooms	Hang lamps, rugs, blankets, tapestries, or large pictures
	Hang a wall shelf to imitate a mantel
Bricked-up fireplace	Hang a mantel and install a metal "cover" where the fireplace opening should be
	Construct an imitation hearth by laying bricks without mortar, keeping them in place by a length of quarter-round
Missing pocket doors	Hang portieres (heavy curtains), suspended by wooden rings from a heavy wooden rod
Missing ceiling lights	Install overhead fans
	Hang wall shelves to accommodate appropriately styled lamps, such as wired oil lamps
	Mount stained glass offset from walls, with lights behind the glass
	Use painting lights to illuminate wall hangings

Problem	Penny-Pincher solution
No closet space	Build large, free-standing wardrobes
	Use camelback and wardrobe trunks freely for additional storage
	Develop attic or basement for long-term storage space

What to Restore—What to Improve —What to Remodel

The question of what to improve, what to restore, and what to renovate is a difficult one. The answers to it are almost as many as there are restorers and renovators. Even historic preservationists, who spend weeks looking for authentic nails and carefully excavate layers of paint to find original colors, have to make decisions about what to improve and remodel. Any house from the nineteenth century that has a bathroom has most likely already been improved, and most old houses have been somewhat remodeled during their history. Sometimes one finds a 100-year-old Victorian era house that was remodeled six or seven decades ago into a perfectly charming and very valuable English Tudor, the merit of which is not diminished by the renovation.

The terms remodel, renovate, and restore have very specific meanings. *Remodeling* implies modernizing a room or house with the intent of making it more attractive, convenient, and comfortable, but not necessarily conforming to the style of the original. *Renovation* means to improve an older structure while at the same time maintaining some of its original character. The word "reviving" in the title of this book is most closely akin to "renovating." *Restoration* is the most particular and specific of the three, and means an attempt to replicate the original structure exactly, whether or not it is convenient and appropriate to modern life. The following guidelines might help the beginning renovator:

Restore
• What is within reach financially and practically
• Items that have to do with the exterior appearance
• Architectural features that have to do with the interior appearance
• Visible features that especially delight you
• Items that will not require the destruction of perfectly sound

improvements of a former owner
- Items, the restoration of which will not create major and continuing maintenance problems

Improve
- All systems, such as plumbing, heating, and electric, when they require replacement
- Invisible construction details
- Strategic matters of convenience
- Insulation and other features that will prevent heat loss and adequate cooling
- Those areas that will dramatically reduce energy and maintenance costs
- Paints, putty, fillers, papers, varnishes, and floor coverings

Remodel
- What you perceive was inexpressibly ugly even when it was new
- What has been irrevocably and poorly remodeled by former owners
- Areas and details that are not the primary focus of the house visually and that will not change its identity

Seven Ways to Destroy Your House
1. Modernize or reduce the size of a porch
2. Screen and, especially, enclose a porch
3. Install modern and/or smaller windows than the original
4. Modernize the main entrance doorway
5. Add any kind of artificial siding
6. Lower a high ceiling
7. Divide rooms

Information Resources
You need not know everything about renovation, but you should learn where you can find information about specific problems or techniques as the need arises. Here are some of the places to start:
- How-to books on specific skills, such as
  - Carpentry
  - Plumbing
  - Electrical wiring
  - Heating

- General books on remodeling, renovation, and restoration
- Journals and magazines
- Building supplies people
- Other home renovators
- Your own observation of
  - Construction projects
  - Local restoration efforts
  - Historic districts in other communities
- Old house and garden magazines from the era of your house and the twenty years following (find them in public and college libraries)

Careful planning and recordkeeping not only can save you hours and days of precious time but they also can help you keep costs as low, and as manageable for your resources, as possible. Use the suggestions in this chapter to
- Make your lists of priorities
- Make good photographs and drawings of your house
- Consider alternative timesaving and/or money-saving solutions to problems
- Evaluate the extent of renovating or restoring really necessary
- Arm yourself with as much information about all aspects of your project as you can muster

With all of this in hand, you are now ready to get down to work.

Tools

As you approach this project of house revival, you will need a few tools beyond that marvelous collection consisting of a one-clawed hammer, a broken screwdriver, a bent ice pick, and malfunctioning pliers that you may remember from your Aunt Mamie's kitchen drawer. With those she seemed able to nail together, take apart, or pry open anything she desired, but that was her special gift. You probably aren't gifted in quite the same sense that Aunt Mamie was, and, besides, the job that you intend to do is most likely more sophisticated and more ambitious, and there are certain basic carpenter tools that are fairly essential if you are going to do a passable job. Perhaps one or two of these things may be just my cranky old idea of what you need, but for the most part I think you will find these useful.

Basic Carpenter Tools

- Handsaw
- Hammer
- Screwdrivers and chisels
- Tape measure or folding rule
- Framing square, with both 16- and 24-inch blades
- Combination square that makes both 45° and 90° angles
- A 2- and/or a 4-foot level
- Nail sets of varying sizes
- Utility knife with replaceable blades
- Carpenter's scriber, or pencil compass

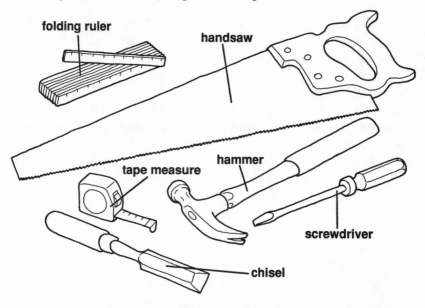

Sometimes you will be able to find old, secondhand tools (particularly saws) that are better than inexpensive, poor-quality new ones. Be sure not to choose a kinked, or warped, *handsaw*, which you can spot by looking in a straight line down the teeth. The time-honored standards in handsaws are, for rough work, an 8-point saw and for finish work, a 10-point (referring to points per inch).

I prefer wooden handled *hammers* because if the handle breaks, it can be replaced. Some people keep a lightweight (12- or 14-ounce) hammer for finish work, but I find that having one this light causes me to make mistakes. A 16-ounce hammer is standard for general work. If you get a bigger hammer for rough work, make sure it is one that you can control; some would tire out a world-class

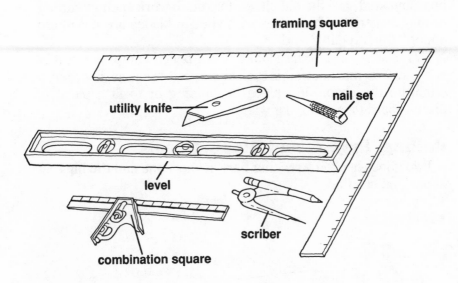

framing square

utility knife

nail set

level

scriber

combination square

arm wrestler who used them very much.

Get what you can in *screwdrivers* and *chisels*, but don't spend all your nickels on them. It's good to have at least three chisels: a 1/2-inch and a 3/4-inch chisel, plus an extra of any size for rough work. Most important: Keep your chisels sharp.

In *measuring tools*, the choice is largely between metal tape measures and folding wooden rules. Some folks prefer tape measures, but the wooden folding rules are the time-honored standard of the carpenter and a pleasure to use. Keep the blade on the tape or the joints on the folding rule oiled.

If you buy *squares* secondhand, always check their accuracy. To prove that the tool has not been bent out of square, use it to trace a large square with a sharp pencil on a piece of paper or plywood. The line for the final side should end at exactly the beginning point for the first side.

To check the accuracy of your *level*, draw a horizontal line on a wall with the bubble showing level. Next, with the side of the level that was against the wall now facing you, draw a second line right beside the first line. The two lines should be exactly parallel. Do the same thing drawing vertical lines.

A *nail set* is a punch designed to set nails below the surface.

The *utility knife* is sometimes referred to as a box cutter and has blades similar to razor blades. It is the only thing made that does a good job cutting wallboard. Keep a sharp blade in it for wall-boarding, and save the old blades for rough work such as cutting roofing material. The knives with slide-in blades are not tough enough for carpentry work.

The *carpenter's scriber* looks like a pencil compass but it is shorter. You must have this tool, or a pencil compass, in order to duplicate the shape of a piece of molding or to fit a piece of plasterboard to an irregular wall.

Pulling, Prying, and Ripping Tools

- Two goose-necked wrecking bars, a short one and the biggest one you can find
- Pry bar
- Nail puller

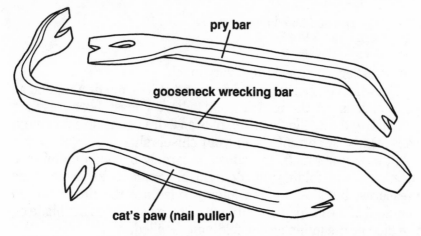

pry bar

gooseneck wrecking bar

cat's paw (nail puller)

The heavy-duty *wrecking bar* will be a magic tool when you need to tear things apart. Use this, instead of a hammer, when you need to pull nails.

The *pry bar* is shaped like a wrecking bar except that it is flat and about 1 1/2 inches wide by 1/8 inch thick. It is surely one of the most wonderful tools ever invented. For years I had used a couple of old tire irons until I discovered that these pry bars are as much better than my old tire irons as a Rolls Royce is better than a motorbike. Be sure you buy a good one, for, because of its small dimensions, it must be tempered very well if it is to withstand the stress you will require of it. Use it for prying off moldings, lifting up wallboard with your foot while you hold the board in place with your chin and nail with your hands, and for many similar jobs.

A *nail puller* is a heavy iron gadget about 18 inches long. To operate it, you place its two little jaws on each side of a nail head, then slam down the pounding mechanism driving the jaws into the wood beneath the nail head. After that, you use it like a regular wrecking bar or the claws of a hammer to pull the nail out. I bought mine thirty years ago and have found it indispensable.

Other Helpful Tools

You probably already own many other helpful tools, and you may be forced to add one or more others as particular jobs pose special needs. These might include

- Self-contained chalk line
- Carpenter's axe
- Hand sledge and sledge hammer
- Vise
- Sawhorses
- Long surveyor's tape
- Block plane
- Smooth and/or jack plane
- Tack hammer
- Sliding T-bevel (for capturing angles other than 45° and 90°)
- Tin snips
- Stapler
- Putty knife
- Broad knife (4- and 8-inch) (looks like a wide putty knife)
- Pocket knife
- Vise grips

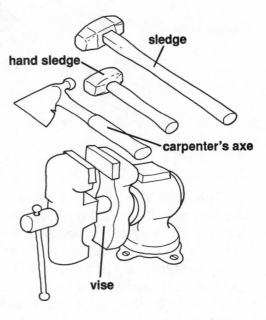

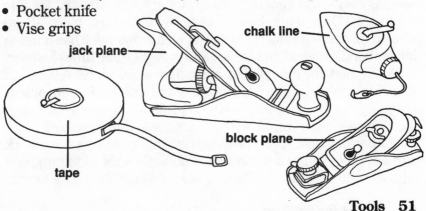

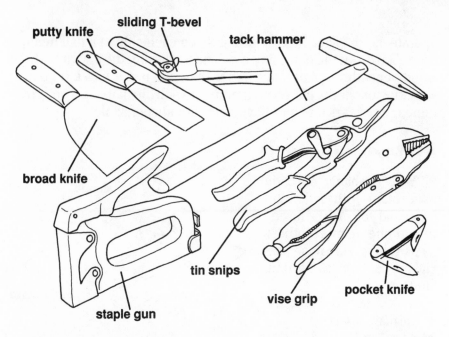

putty knife

sliding T-bevel

tack hammer

broad knife

tin snips

staple gun

vise grip

pocket knife

The *chalk line* is needed when you are trying to mark the location of joists or studs behind your wallboard or for getting a straight starting line for roofing or siding. The line is chalked as it is pulled out. You then put it in place, draw it tight, and snap it.

A *carpenter's axe* is indispensable to me. Used with care, it serves as a heavy hammer (watch it though, you can cut yourself badly on the back swing), a stake maker, or a tool for cutting things down to size.

A *hand sledge* with a 10-inch handle is very useful. You should keep one, however, only if you know that you are absolutely free from the tendency to see a bigger hammer as the ultimate solution to every difficulty. For instance, a hand sledge is not used to make big things fit into too-small places. (Conversely, it is a pity that no one has ever made a good board stretcher for boards that are just a bit short. Do-it-yourselfers—not to say also, carpenters—have wished for them for many years.) A sledge hammer has a much longer handle than a hand sledge and is about three times heavier.

A *vise* might be mounted on a bench or a sawhorse. A friend of mine has one bolted on a 3-foot piece of 4x8 so that it is more or less portable. An iron carpenter's vise is probably more useful than a wooden one, but it would be really convenient to have both.

Rather than use your grandmother's antique chair for a work surface, build yourself some *sawhorses* with fairly wide tops, and with legs either splayed or built like an old-fashioned park bench.

In the latter case, make them of 12-inch stock, low enough so that you can comfortably and securely hold a board with your knee while you saw it.

Power Tools

- Electric drill
- High quality bits, including wood bits
- Portable jigsaw
- Portable circular saw
- Grinder or belt sander
- Cordless screwdriver
- Reciprocal saw
- Table or radial arm saw

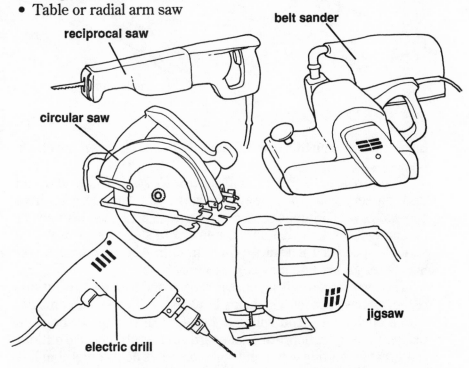

reciprocal saw

belt sander

circular saw

electric drill

jigsaw

The *drill* and *jigsaw* can be cheap. Often you will find them on sale around Father's Day. Just having the tool is nine-tenths of the benefit—the other tenth is the quality of your particular model. If you can afford a little bit better grade, buy a medium-priced *circular saw,* for it will usually get the hardest wear of all the tools mentioned here. The next tool to upgrade would be the *disk sander*, in order to get one with more power. You may sometimes

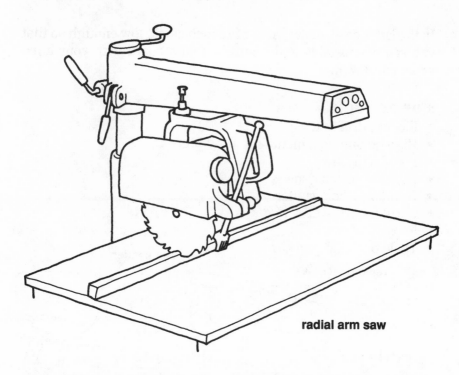

radial arm saw

have reason to run this continuously and this is hard on the cheap ones.

If you are able to get a *reversible, variable-speed drill*, you would find it a very good investment, because you can use it to drive screws. Special Phillips screws are made to be driven with power equipment, but it is also possible to put in slotted screws with a variable-speed drill if it will go slow enough. A *cordless screwdriver* is another luxury you may come to crave.

The *reciprocal saw* is one of the most wonderful tool inventions of the last few decades and, to my knowledge, no one has come out with a cheap one. You will use a reciprocal saw to cut holes in plaster walls, or in floors or baseboards to install electrical outlets. It is great for cutting water and soil pipes. It is held something like a tommy gun with the blade coming out of the end where the bullets would spray.

Both *table* and *radial arm saws* make using salvage materials easier because you can rip up boards into any size you need. With the radial arm saw you move the blade over the board, whereas with the table saw you move the board over the blade. A *grinder* or a *belt sander* is also helpful to have. To save money, you could use a rubber tie-down to strap a portable disk sander to a bench or stand and use it as you would a stationary sander or grinder for sharpening tools.

All of these power tools are a delight to own, but they may represent a large investment of your resources, too, so hold off on them unless you are lucky enough to find inexpensive, or better yet, free ones.

Outdoor Equipment
- Wheelbarrow
- Shovel
- Pick
- Digging bar

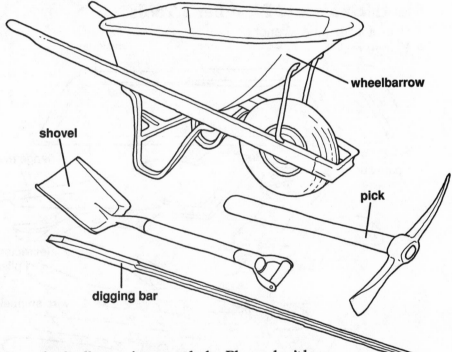

A *wheelbarrow* is a great help. Please don't buy one of those little things that are hard to distinguish from a child's toy. Get a contractor's wheelbarrow, and you'll be glad you did. Similarly, buy a good *shovel* and a good, heavy-duty *pick*.

A *digging bar*, once called a crowbar, is an important tool, and one you may be lucky to find secondhand. The heavier it is, the better. They were once produced commercially for use as levers to move big crates in warehouses. I've got a homemade one fashioned out of an axle from a piece of old farm machinery. Recently a blacksmith friend re-pointed it by heating it red hot with a welding torch, hammering it to a chisel point on an anvil, and plunging it into a plastic milk carton full of old motor oil to re-temper it.

Whether homemade or commercially manufactured, digging bars are a marvelous aid for digging holes, starting a hole for a stake, prying things off a wall, ripping up sidewalks, and the like. Old-time ditchdiggers and grave diggers would have never thought of starting a hole without a digging bar; and when the job was complete, the sides were so straight that the hole might have been sawed out.

Electrician's and Plumber's Tools

- Pair of large pipe wrenches
- Flange maker

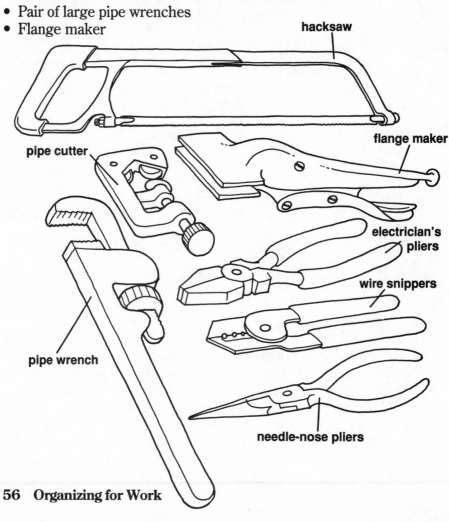

hacksaw

flange maker

pipe cutter

electrician's pliers

wire snippers

pipe wrench

needle-nose pliers

- Tubing cutter
- Electrician's pliers
- Needle-nose pliers
- Wire strippers
- Hacksaw
- Flashlight

Pipe wrenches are always needed in a set of two, because you secure the pipe with one and remove the fitting with the other. If you are going to do any plumbing with plastic pipe, you can probably borrow pipe wrenches for the few times you will need them.

If you are going to do a lot of work with copper tubing, you will need to buy a *propane torch, flange maker*, and a *tubing cutter*, but you probably can find a local hardware store that cuts tubing to order.

Painter's Tools

- Brushes
- Roller

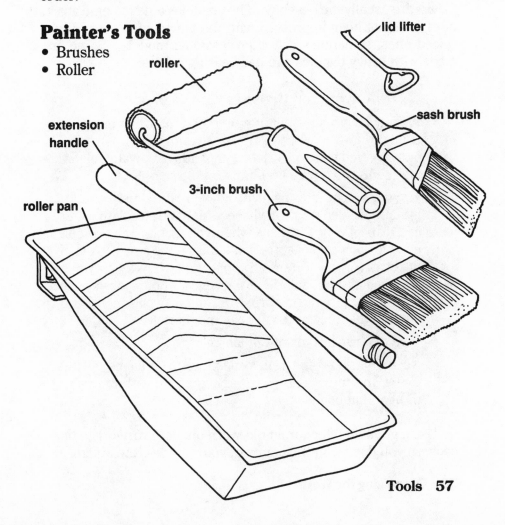

lid lifter

roller

sash brush

extension handle

3-inch brush

roller pan

- Roller pan
- Extension handle
- Lid lifter
- Stepladder
- Extension ladder
- Tarps

Good-quality *brushes* are a necessity. Some people think they can't paint, but the real truth is that they can't paint with the awful brushes they have always tried to use. For a good start, you will need 4-inch and 3-inch all-purpose brushes and a 1-inch sash brush. Get a *paint roller* and *pan* as well as an *extension handle for the roller*. Both ceilings and walls are much easier to paint if you can stand on the floor rather than on a ladder.

If you buy the cheapest paint rollers on sale, you can throw them out at the end of the particular job. Medium-priced roller *frames* are usually the best buy. The cheapies tend to come apart, but I have not been impressed with the advantages of the high-priced ones, sometimes called professional models. Some are made with heavy handles and ball-bearing rollers.

Caring for Brushes and Rollers

- Wash your brushes out in mineral spirits when using oil paint or in water when using latex paint, then wash them out very well in laundry detergent and warm water, cleaning them with a wire brush.

- If you are using latex paint, do not store the brush or roller in water to keep it soft; it will become saturated with water and drip all over the place when you use it again. If you need to apply two coats of paint, it isn't necessary to clean the brush or roller between applications, however, even if the second coat isn't done for several hours or several days. Instead, wrap the brush or roller in a plastic bag and put it in the freezer; it will keep indefinitely.

- Save old brushes for rough jobs.

- No matter how the roller mechanism attaches to the frame, the thing tends to get clogged up with old paint right at that point.

Use a good lid lifter (or an old worn-out screwdriver) to open cans, so you don't ruin the points of your good screwdrivers.

You need a couple of *stepladders* and an *extension ladder.* ("You can never have too much money or too many ladders," the expression goes.)

A good *canvas tarp* (or several of them) is helpful, but you can always use plastic drop cloths or old bedspreads or sheets. I think plastic sheeting as a floor cover is a pain in the neck because it absorbs nothing and you are thus apt to track wet paint all over the house. Plastic sheeting *is* useful to cover up furniture, appliances, or radiators during painting. Just remember to handle it carefully if you remove it before the paint dries. Paint tends to stay in a liquid state longer on the plastic than on the wall and it's easy to spread it around. The advantage of a canvas tarp is that unlike bedspreads and sheets it won't leak and yet unlike plastic cloths it is absorbent. "The bigger the better" is the rule in tarps. Half the burden of painting is that you really need to be able to wrap things up well and cover up a large area. A common problem of amateur painters is that they are inadequately equipped with drop cloths and thus may either slop paint all over everything or else take forever and a day to paint one room.

Where and How to Get Tools to Restore Your House
- Purchase new only as a last resort
- Basements and garages of relatives or friends who no longer use them
- Classified advertisements
- Flea markets
- Household auctions and estate sales
- Secondhand stores and pawn shops
- Retired builders
- Bought with your house

Some Precautions to Keep Tools from Ruining Your Life

Tools have a way of doing that to some people. The situation is something like a poor man who wins the lottery, after which the proceeds in one way or another begin to take over his life. Tools are your servants, not your masters, and you must keep them that way. Here are some general rules and cautions having to do with your collection of tools.

- Don't become a tool "freak"; you are renovating a house not collecting tools.

- You need good tools, of course, but not necessarily the best ones.
- Avoid letting antique tool collecting become a fad. Buy old when you can, but do not put all your means into tools.
- Accept all gifts and inheritances.
- Keep your tools clean, sharp, and otherwise in good condition.
- Keep your tools hung up or on shelves. Boxes are good only if you have a problem with security and safety in your work area.
- Make a carrying box to take with you to the location of the job.
- When you have finished a job, put your tools away.
- Take a little time at the end of each work session to pick up wood and paper scraps and just generally neaten the work site. You'll feel much more like returning to the job if things are not a mess.

Collecting Old-House Treasure

Every renovator needs a treasure room. When the pharaohs of ancient Egypt built their pyramids, they always built a room to fill with inexpressibly rich treasures, stored up for the next life. Your treasure room is in view of a much nearer afterlife, for it will contain all the things you can store up that you will eventually use to renovate your grand old house. It may be a barn, a large room in your house, or even an attic, if there is good access. A friend of mine has a 200-foot chicken house filled with rich treasure. The treasure room needs to be dry and well lighted. It may also serve as a workshop and will at least be a place for you to keep your tools. But it is primarily a place for storing the treasure you need to renovate your home if you are going to be able to do so on a shoestring budget.

Some of the things you put in your treasure room will someday be virtually priceless. These include

- Old doors
- Windows
- Doorknobs
- Porch balustrades
- Porch and stair balusters
- Mantels
- Moldings

In many cases you would have a hard time buying these for any price at a minute's notice, and in months and years to come they may be harder to find than they are now. I am struck with how often it happens that someone tells me that such-and-such an item is very scarce and very expensive, and I am reminded that at one time I could have had several or a dozen of them for the mere carrying away. I once carried porch balusters for more than a thousand miles and then kept them for nearly a decade when they became an essential ingredient in a sleeping balcony I was building. Right now, I wish I had twenty or thirty more balusters to build a round turret at the end of my porch.

Your treasure room will also have more ordinary possessions. Your primary purpose is to gather items you will eventually need for some large or small work of restoration or unanticipated repair, organized into cans of old screws, old bolts and nuts, and nails arranged by sizes. You'll also need a place for paint storage and a place for leftover wood and other building supplies. Your collection might include

- Boards
- Studs and planks
- Nails
- Hinges
- Screws
- Bolts and nuts
- Plywood (substantial pieces only)
- Insulation board
- Glass
- Pipes
- Vents
- Heat registers

You will surely include leftovers from other projects. Every time you buy nails for a specific job, you might have from a handful to several pounds left over. If you mix them up or leave them all over, they are almost useless and you will use four times your allotted share of nails for your lifetime. And have you ever tried to buy one screw to replace the one that has broken on a door hinge? In most stores, instead of one screw, you will have to buy a little pasteboard card containing four screws, costing about a third of what a box of 100 screws would cost in an old-fashioned hardware store. If you have a treasure room, you'll have twelve screws you took out of another door you removed the week before. You can probably cut your small parts bill by 80 percent in one year if you have a well-stocked treasure room.

Treasure Room Rules

If you are to have a real treasure room and not a mere replication of the city dump, you will need to follow a few rules.

Keep your treasure room orderly. The pharaohs could dump their gold into their treasure rooms in lavish disarray, but they did not intend to have mortals rooting around in them looking for spare parts. Your purpose is to be able to use your treasure in this life. You need to be able to find a piece of pipe or a doorbell someone gave you so you can put it into use. If you do not exercise discipline, your collection will surely descend to chaos.

To this end it is well worth your time and expense to look for some metal or wooden shelves. You will want to have a section

for paint and separate places for lumber, nails, tools, hardware, and the like. I like to use plastic dishpans for bins to store loose items on the shelves. If you can get some metal shelves, they will be excellent because they will not rot nor succumb to termites— nor be a temptation when you think you'd give almost anything for the right-size board, and the right-size board is exactly the same dimensions as your shelf board. In a pinch, some old planks laid on cement blocks make an adequate shelving system, though cement blocks have become expensive. Be sure to leave lots of space for growth so that you do not have to rear-

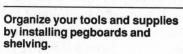

Organize your tools and supplies by installing pegboards and shelving.

range things continually as you add to your collection.

Periodically spend time cleaning up and throwing out.
Dismantle as much as possible. Usually you will want only a small
part of every piece of junk you collect. Don't waste your space by
saving it all. Throw away what is useless. There are things that you
will never use. Throw them out. Like all the rest of us treasure
keepers, your temptation will be to keep everything. Throw away:
- Used nails
- Short and irregular pieces of wood and plywood
- All but whole sheets of wallboard
- Old wire
- Old electrical fixtures (unless antique)
- Dried out paint cans

Find room for fresh treasure not yet stowed away. So that the
half dozen shutters and a porch swing someone gave you don't end
up on your front porch or in the hall, sewing room, or bathtub, you
will need a temporary place for your treasures until you put them
in permanent storage or in place on the house.

Keep your room safe, sanitary, and respectable. It must not
be a haven for rats, roaches, opossums, termites, or other freeloaders, such as the neighbor's cat. Some of the above rules will
help.

Reserve space for a work area on a cold day. You will need
to paint, strip furniture, build cabinets, rebuild shutters, or putty
windows somewhere, and, especially in inclement weather, this
may be the best place to do it, here in the midst of your tools and
treasure. If you have managed things right, this will be one of the
happy places in your house to spend an afternoon or an evening
doing something useful, while passing the hours in deep and
profound contemplation.

Such a treasure room—organized, well-kept, sensible, and
disciplined—will be a source of incalculable savings and personal
satisfaction. It will also make you a favored friend among other
renovators, restorers, and remodelers, and able to call in an
unlimited number of IOUs when you, too, need spare parts or a
spare hand.

Pre-used Materials; or, One Person's Trash is Another Person's Treasure

One of the major ways you can pinch pennies is to use second-hand materials. This assumes, of course, that you have the time to invest in their procurement. But remember, there is an ultimate economy in investing hours instead of dollars in your house. *Find time!* You'll be glad you did. This is one reason to prioritize and to put off labor on unnecessary things in order to buy time to collect free materials.

Hassles with Pre-used Materials

- Storage (they look like trash—and your neighbors may think so, too)
- Huge time investment in their procurement
- Danger in their procurement
- Transportation back to your house
- Harder to work with than new materials

Benefits in Pre-used Materials

- Usually free for the carrying away, or at least a tremendous savings
- Source of invaluable material often impossible to buy elsewhere at any price
- Often better material than new
- Sizes match old sizes (for example, framing lumber)
- Ecologically responsible

The benefits clearly outweigh the hassle. Storage is not so much a problem as it might seem. If the only place to store your materials is outside, polyethylene tarps with fibers embedded in them (the ubiquitous blue tarps that you see everywhere) are cheap, tough, incredibly long-lasting, and absolutely waterproof. Time spent procuring free material is no hassle at all and can save you thousands of dollars on the cost of renovation. You may even be able to sell some of your finds to other renovators. You will get your reward for the time and trouble when you see a beautiful floor laid out of 100-year-old hard pine, with its beautiful dark red color showing a richness that is not seen in any new wood, no matter what kind of stain or finish is used to treat it.

To obtain materials at no cost, you may have to
- Agree to remove a house or barn
- Enter into a cooperative venture with another renovator
- Get permission from an owner or contractor to salvage materials before scheduled building demolition
- Get permission from the owner of an abandoned building to take specific parts

Often it is easier than it might seem. Owners or contractors who are going to tear down or burn a building will often see your request to take some of their materials, as a small amount of help in carrying the pile of junk away. For example, a builder friend of mine helped me acquire a huge load of 2x4s, as well as other almost-new materials from a large deck he had just demolished in order to build an insulated sunroom for a client. An unbreakable rule in getting freebies like this is, "Take what you can get and take *everything* that you get." The first time you turn down a load of junk that a well-meaning friend has gone to the trouble to save for you, you will begin to cut off your supply.

"Free" Houses

You might even get a surprisingly good, complete house without cost, although often "free" houses are of poor quality. Because of the high cost of tearing down a building commercially, an owner may want to get rid of it badly enough to be willing for you to get the whole thing on the ground and reduced to scraps, after which he will pay for the final clean-up himself. If it is a very good house, you might have to pay a few hundred dollars for it. In that case, however, there probably will be some goodies to sell that will repay the investment manyfold.

On occasion, business concerns give houses away to anyone who will move them in order to avoid blame for destroying an old building. A number of fine buildings have been given away by churches in our area for this reason. If you run across a building that no one is willing to move, it could be an excellent house to tear down and well worth your time.

Problems Encountered in Tearing Down a Building

Safety is the first concern. Extreme care should be the byword for all demolition activities. Good shoes (never tennis or running shoes) and a hard hat are the dress code. A tetanus shot within the last ten years is imperative, as is, also, a good health insurance policy. Demolition is dangerous. But then, it is no more dangerous than boating, football, or hunting, if you pay attention to safety.

Looting is a real problem. In many areas—even in areas where there are not many other crimes of theft—they will descend on your house like Attila the Hun and his boys. Several precautions will cut your losses:

- Work from the inside out as much as possible so that you can remove all the goodies before they become exposed. For instance, begin by removing all
    - Brass doorknobs
    - Chandeliers
    - Good bathroom fixtures
    - Valuable windows and doors, especially leaded-glass windows
    - Mantels
    - Staircases
- Board up open windows and doors when you leave the site.
- Carry away everything that is loose.
- Ask the police and the neighbors to watch the house.
- Attach "No Trespassing" signs to dramatize that the site is not a community free-for-all.

Clean up is the big problem of demolition, unless you have been given permission to take what you want before a contractor runs through the remains with a bulldozer. Obviously, not many people are going to give or sell you a house and then allow you to leave the site looking like a war zone. In rural areas, you may be able to burn the building. Check first with the local fire department, and then take extreme precautions against grass or forest fires. Some fire departments welcome a chance to hold a fire drill at such an event. They may ask for a small donation, but often they'll burn an old building down for no charge. You'll still have a lot of trash to haul off if you burn it first, but it will certainly be reduced.

On the other hand, you might contract with an earth-moving or grading contractor to break up the remains before burying or hauling them off some place. If you can make arrangements to dump on some nearby lot where they need fill, you will save a lot of money on the deal. If there is a cellar hole under the building, it may be possible to push the rubble into the hole and cover it up with dirt. Selling a small part of the materials you have garnered from this house might pay for this clean up.

What to Save

- Timbers
- Foundation sills
- Framing lumber
- Boards
- Windows and doors
- Window and door frames
- Siding (even if only the reverse face is acceptable)
- Molding
- Flooring
- Trim boards
- Hardware
- Chandeliers
- Lighting fixtures and parts
- Mantels
- Bricks
- Tiles
- Stairway parts
- Stair balustrades and newel post
- Window seats
- Bay windows (mark them before disassembling)
- Plumbing fixtures
- Shutters
- Porch posts
- Porch balustrades or balusters
- All decoration, interior or exterior

Storage of a Disassembled House

Very few renovators have the luxury of covered storage for the huge amount of materials a disassembled house provides, so you will most likely store them outdoors. Normally you should plan to stack them where you will not have to move them.

- Arrange your storage pile neatly by categories.
- Remove all nails.
- Use cross pieces (called *stickers*) between lumber every so often to provide
    - Ventilation
    - Warp-free storage
    - Easier access

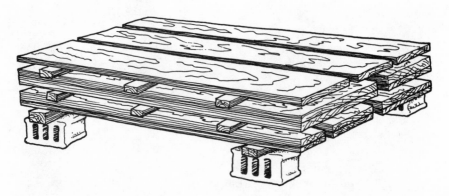

Stack lumber using stickers every so often to provide ventilation and easier access, and to prevent warping.

- Keep things up off the ground (put cross pieces on cement blocks).
- Never put wooden materials on the ground, where bugs, snails, and other creepie-crawlies will turn the pile into a condo.
- Cover materials with large, reinforced polyethylene tarp, tied at the corners to cement blocks so you can move the blocks to borrow from or add to the pile.

Moving a House, or Part of a House

In certain situations you might consider moving a house to use as an additional wing to your present house or as the main house, with your present house made into a guest house. You can find these bargains by watching legal and classified advertisements in your newspaper.

Often, houses that must be moved are free, or surprisingly inexpensive, often, as I have said, because an owner is faced with negative public opinion or really would prefer not to destroy a lovely old house. The small price for the house itself is deceptive, however, because there is considerable cost to moving a house. Even so, it is often a great bargain.

House moving is a task for a professional. Nearly always, the local authorities will require proof of insurance on the part of the mover. The cost of the moving is based upon how low to the ground are the power lines, how wide are the streets, and whether the house to be moved is located near the new site, or at least near an open street that is a clear shot to the new site.

In cities, the second story is almost always removed, after being carefully marked for rebuilding. Sometimes a large house is cut down through the middle to get the portions into street-sized units. In other houses, appendages are removed, according to the structure of the house, determined by the framing under the first floor. One of these appendages removed from someone else's house-moving project might be your best bargain. Often for a small amount of cash, house movers can get one of these on a flat-bed trailer and move it to your lot for a new wing on your old house.

In rural areas, or in cities where there is no problem with trees or wires overhead, it is not uncommon to move the whole house—porches, roof, plumbing, and kitchen cupboards—all in one piece. Even so, porch roofs need to be shored up with braces going from the side of the main building and foundations removed in order to get the iron beams under the house, and, later, to allow the house and its supporting beams to roll away on its journey to a new address.

Another way to move a house is to mark it, take it apart, and reassemble it. Ordinarily, one does not mark each single piece, since all the rafters are presumably the same and the floors and decking on the roof could be put back together in any order. In any case, make a good set of drawings of the house before tearing things apart or you might find that all the king's horses and all the king's men can't tell this pile of lumber from a jigsaw puzzle.

Whether you are looking for materials and supplies, or searching for an entire building, with a bit of patience, hard work, and organization you can collect what you need for little, if any, cost. Arrange a place to store your finds, be ever on the lookout for possibilities, keep your treasures organized and manageable, and observe commonsense safety rules, and your savings and resources will mount.

4

WEATHERIZATION AND EXTERIOR REVIVAL

Weatherization for Your Old House

A part of what we mean by our word "home" is a shelter that to some extent protects us from the elements and provides the kind of environment we need or desire on the inside. Keeping the outdoors out-of-doors without sacrificing the beauty of your old house presents special challenges. This section has to do with the insulation and the exterior of your house, the only things between you and the weather.

It is very rare that you will find an old house that does not need a great deal of attention to insulation and other energy conservation measures. A first step may be merely to keep the wind from roaring through the various cracks and holes so much that the curtains blow in the breeze. All old houses need to be better insulated than they were designed to be, but there's no truth to the myth that this lack of insulation means that one can't live comfortably and economically in an old house and that they are all doomed to be torn down. Granting that there are many heat-loss features in an old house that you can do little about, you must be very serious about the kinds of things you *can* do something about.

The main reason buildings from the last century were not insulated is that few good insulating materials were available. But over time, other problems may have exacerbated this lack of thermal integrity, even in the best of old houses:

- Building may have been constructed carelessly.
- Old-style windows run well but seal poorly.
- Warping has caused cracks in the exterior.
- Interior plaster, which was the major sealing material, has cracked.
- Rot, termites, or squirrels have made holes.
- A careless remodeling effort was undertaken.

How Our Ancestors Coped with Cold Weather

For homemade insulation, the old-timers sometimes used crunched up newspapers, dirt, corn cobs, or aged manure, all of which had decided disadvantages. Layers of wood and plaster were better, but of minimal insulating value. Sawdust, although effective, encouraged rodents, snakes, and rot. The best ways of dealing with the cold were to add more wood or coal to the fire, put on more clothes, and simply huddle around the heat source and pray for an early spring. And in some cases, insulation just wasn't considered worth much trouble, because most people had cheap heat.

Special Cooling Features in Old Houses

Our ancestors' dwellings dealt somewhat more effectively with hot summers. The following typical features, in fact, are some of the real assets of an older home:
- Double-hung windows that open top and bottom
- Shutters that let the air in but keep the sun out
- High ceilings
- Central halls with doors front and back
- Houses built on piers (in the South)
- Houses built in groves of trees (especially in the South)
- Detached kitchens (especially in the South)

Modern Weatherization Materials

Some modern methods have proved to have problems of their own. Asbestos, which was poured or blown into the walls (see pages 27-28), and a foam containing formaldehyde have both been found to be carcinogenic. There are some relatively inexpensive and simple insulation techniques, however, that work quite well. Small areas or cracks may be insulated or plugged with an aerosol urethane foam or with latex or, better still, silicone caulking material. Temporary, inexpensive sealing can be accomplished with polyethylene sheeting. Serious consideration should be given to those projects and methods that offer the most gain.

Degrees of Gain in Weatherization

High Yield	Medium Yield	Small Yield
Ceiling insulation	Wall insulation	Floor insulation
Stopping up large air leaks, such as chimney openings	Storm windows	Weather stripping
	Stopping up small air leaks	Reglazing windows
		Caulking exterior around edges of windows

Methods of Insulating Ceilings

Method	Advantages	Disadvantages
Blown-in ceiling insulation	Cheap	Settles as time passes
	Good insulation	Settles quickly if it is disturbed
	Rented machine is operated from outside house, feeding hose in through the attic	Tends to gather moisture
	Can be added to in future	
Fiberglass bats	Moisture-resistant Permanent	More expensive May be difficult to get material into attic
	Contains a moisture-barrier paper	
	Can be added to	

Methods of Insulating Walls

Methods	Advantages	Disadvantages
Blown-in insulation	Cheap Relatively easy	Unless a vapor barrier is applied to interior walls, moisture will build up behind exterior siding, causing mold and poor paint retention on siding Occasional air pockets or other unfilled areas Settles as it gets older
Fiberglass bats	Good coverage Minimal moisture problems No settling	Expensive and time-consuming because it requires the removal of interior walls for installation
Rigid foam sheathing	To some extent, forms its own vapor barrier between interior of room and siding	Expensive Necessitates rebuilding interior walls Because it is flammable, it *must* be covered with wallboard that is *at least* 1/2 inch thick, for fire protection.

An excellent option for a major renovation effort is to tear out all the plaster and lath on outside walls, apply rigid foam sheathing or fiberglass bats between studs, and cover insulation with wall-

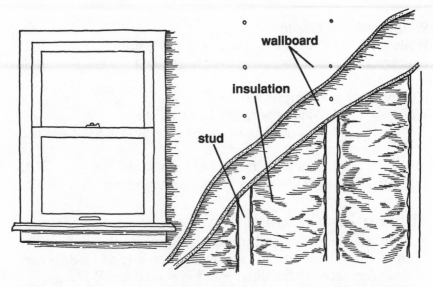

This cutaway shows new bat insulation between studs, covered by two layers of wallboard to bring wall out approximately to its original level

board—two thicknesses, if necessary, to build the wall out to its original thickness so that the old woodwork will show properly. If you decide on this course, you can also take the opportunity, while the walls are open, to upgrade wiring and to remove window casings and make any necessary repairs to decaying sash cords.

The much easier way is to add rigid foam insulation right over the existing plaster, then a layer of wallboard over that for a fresh wall surface. Window casings have to be made even deeper. New baseboards must be used.

Rigid foam sheathing is flammable and thus must be covered by 1/2-inch wallboard or another thermal barrier approved by local buildng codes.

Measurement of Insulation

The government-set standard of measurement for all insulation is the "R-value," invariably marked right on the insulation.

Insulation Efficiency Ratings

Adequately Insulated Home

Walls	3 1/2-inch fiberglass between the studs	R-16
Ceilings	5 1/2-inch fiberglass over the ceiling	R-16

Well-Insulated Home

Walls	3 1/2-inch fiberglass between the studs	R-11
Ceilings	11-inch fiberglass over the ceiling	R-32

Highly Energy-Efficient Home

Walls	3 1/2-inch fiberglass between studs	
	+ 1-inch rigid foam sheathing	R-11 + R-7.2 = R-18.2
	or	
	5 1/2-inch fiberglass between studs	R-16
Ceilings	11-inch fiberglass or more over ceiling	R-32 +

Tips on Insulation

- There are diminishing returns on thicknesses in insulation: The difference in comfort and savings between R-16 and R-32 is very small compared to the difference between 0 and R-16.
- No fair squashing 5 1/2-inch insulation into a 3 1/2-inch area. Although it will have a higher insulating value than 3 1/2-inch insulation in a 3 1/2-inch cavity, its R-value will be less than it would be in a 5 1/2-inch cavity because part of the insulating quality comes from air trapped in the loose fibers.
- Place the paper or aluminum side of insulation, which serves as a vapor barrier to keep moisture away from the insulation material, *toward* the warm side of the house. In other words,

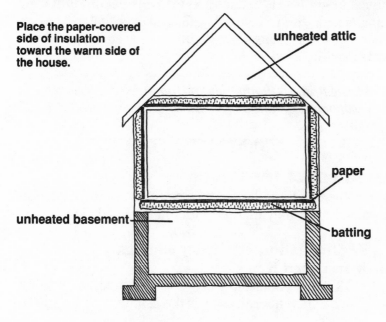

Place the paper-covered side of insulation toward the warm side of the house.

unheated attic

paper

unheated basement

batting

- Toward the room for wall insulation
- Down toward the ceiling below for attic insulation
- Up toward the floor above for basement or crawl space insulation
- You may add a layer of insulation on top of existing insulation that contains a vapor barrier (typically done in the attic); the added insulation should not have a vapor barrier.

How to Use a Cellulose Insulation Blowing Machine

Cellulose insulation must be blown in, rather than poured, because the air that is incorporated during the process fluffs the material up, resulting in greater insulating value. This method works only in buildings that have air spaces between interior walls and exterior siding. An early form of house construction known as the plank house used no such air space; therefore, in these houses rigid foam sheets should be used. The procedure for blown-in insulation is as follows:

- Machines are available at tool rental stores and sometimes at places that sell the insulation. A 50- or 70-foot hose allows you to reach as high as your attic.
- Drill 1- to 1 1/4-inch holes (depending on equipment) between each wall stud both at the top of the wall and just above the foundation, and above and below all windows.
- Blow insulation into upper holes; lower holes both allow air to escape during the insulating process so that no air pockets form, as well as allow you to see whether or not the insulation is filling right to the bottom rather than being blocked by some structural obstruction.
- Examine bottom holes in corners to be certain that insulation fills corners well; sometimes bracing on the interior of the wall blocks the flow at these points.
- Drive plugs cut from wooden dowels and covered with waterproof glue into the holes, and sand surface with disk sander.

Insulation, Moisture, and Proper Ventilation

Peeling paint usually signifies a moisture problem in the present design of the house. Moisture comes from a variety of sources present in any house, not the least of which is condensation formed when the heated air from inside the house meets cold exterior wall surfaces. The places where this meeting occurs, of course, are not only exterior walls, but also ceilings where the area above is unheated and floors where the area below is unheated. Moisture also builds up due to

- Humans (and plants) breathing
- Unvented clothes dryers
- Damp or wet basements or crawl spaces
- Frequent showers
- Cooking
- Roof and gutter leaks

Moisture may build up in one area or in all areas of the house. If it forces its way out through the walls, the exterior paint will mildew and peel. Usually, most is trapped in the attic, where it can run down walls or rot out roof sheathing. Here are some solutions to the problem, in order of their likelihood and importance:

- Cut unnecessary moisture by venting dryer to the outside and placing exhaust fans in bathrooms and kitchen.
- Dry out the basement by improving drainage around the foundation.
- Provide attic ventilation by opening windows, installing turbines on roof, and placing vents in peaks and soffits.
- In bathrooms and kitchens, where a great deal of moisture is generated, apply oil paint or vinyl wallpaper, which will act as an additional vapor barrier.

Plain Talk About Storm Windows and Doors

Storm windows and doors are optional in warm climates, but they become increasingly necessary the farther north and the colder the winter. A good option for old houses, in particular, is to install new double-glazed, small-pane windows. Probably less expensive are aluminum storm windows, but they have disadvantages as well as benefits.

Disadvantages of Aluminum Storm Windows
- They preclude ever again closing the outside shutters over the windows.
- Unless the weight pockets in the window casing can be insulated too, storm windows alone do not provide the incredible results claimed for them.

- Especially if left their natural metal color, they may give a house an undesirably modernized appearance.
- Window cleaning is a difficult chore.
- Two-track storm windows preclude opening upper sash of the original windows for maximum ventilation.

Advantages of Storm Windows
- They save heat in winter and keep an air-conditioned house cooler in summer.
- They present a "clean" look.
- They have very efficient screens.
- They help preserve original sash and sash glazing indefinitely.

Installing Storm Windows
- Glaze and paint the original windows before installing storms. You are wasting your money to add storms to poorly glazed windows that leak air.
- Wash outside of original windows and inside of storms before installation.
- Install windows with screws, never with nails, which will come loose. Cordless screwdrivers are especially nice for this job. If the storm window frame is not prepunched with screw holes, put screws just to the outside of the frame, and angle them away from the window.
- Set frames in a bed of latex caulk.
- Drill drain holes on each side of the frame at the bottom so you do not set up a virtual aquarium between the old window and the storm window.

Restoring Masonry Surfaces and Painting Wood

Masonry houses present very different renovation problems from those of wood houses. Although in most cases, masonry will not need as much attention as a wood exterior, certain problems are fairly common.

Possible Problems with Exterior Masonry

Problem	Probable cause	Solution
Small cracks	Slight settling of foundation	Fill very small cracks with caulk and larger ones with mortar.
Large, new cracks	Ongoing settling: examine the ground around the foundation for puddles or disturbed earth	May be a job for a contractor. Repair gutters and downspouts and be sure water is routed away from house.
Stained masonry	Trees, vines, roof runoff, air pollution	Remove source of problem. Sometimes fresh paint on all woodwork transforms ugly stains into what seems to be a rich patina.
Crumbling mortar	Shrubs or vines too close	Get rid of source of moisture problem.
	Moisture in the wall	Allow wall to dry thoroughly. Tuck-point bad areas.
Eroding bricks	Inferior bricks	Get rid of source of moisture problem.
	Sandblasting	
	Moisture in the wall	

Tuck-pointing

Tuck-pointing is a skill best learned by doing it. You need mortar, a joint tool, a pointing trowel (which looks a bit like a pancake flipper), and a hawk, which is rectangular and unpointed. If you don't have a hawk, use a plastering trowel or a concrete finishing trowel.

Some useful masonry tools can be homemade. For example, take an old screwdriver and bend it into a hook for cleaning out the joints. (Wear protective goggles any time you chip away at mortar.) A joint tool can be made by bending a piece of 1/2-inch copper tubing into a gentle "s."

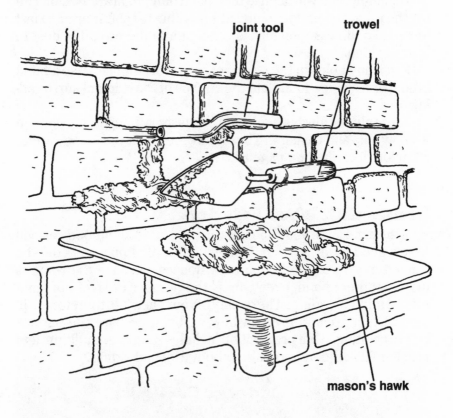

With the trowel, tuck mortar from the mason's hawk into the joint, then remove excess mortar and pack it in using a joint tool.

Steps in Tuck-Pointing

1. Clean out the old mortar somewhat.
2. In a wheelbarrow, or even on a piece of old plywood (a bucket

is less convenient), mix the mortar, using 3 parts sand to 1 part portland cement, plus 10 percent builder's lime. Very gradually add water to obtain a stiff, but not crumbly, mixture. This takes a bit of trial and error, the goal being a mixture that readily packs into the prepared joints.
3. Put mortar on the hawk and hold the hawk just below the joint to be filled.
4. "Tuck" the mortar into the joint with the pointing trowel.
5. "Tool" the joint by rubbing it down to remove excess mortar and then packing down the mortar that remains. This not only gives a nice neat appearance, but it also waterproofs the joint.

Hopefully, you will need to tuck-point only small areas. Don't go overboard in repointing joints. It's possible for soft mortar to last forever, so, unless moisture is running into the wall, it is best to leave it alone.

Patch any holes in the stucco of a stuccoed house. Use a hand broom or a sponge to imitate the surface of the original surrounding area.

Areas almost always neglected on masonry houses are wooden window sills and casings. These must be given the same careful attention described on page 84.

Houses with Wood Exteriors

If the exterior of your house is all wood, in all likelihood you will have a good bit of work to do. Generally, old houses need to be painted more frequently than new houses, because the wood is more weathered and, even worse, the number of layers of paint may be mind-boggling. The quality of your paint job, therefore, will depend to a great degree on how well you prepare the surface before painting. That preparation includes scraping, caulking, and priming, in addition to repairing both trim and siding.

Tips for a Good Paint Job
- Scrape surface properly.
- Clean all grease, dirt, and mold off surfaces.
- If oil paint is used, surface must be completely dry; if latex is used, it must, at least, not be saturated with water. Note manufacturer's advice regarding air temperature; latex should not be applied below certain temperatures, usually about

50°F.
- Caulk any place water could run in.
- Use good-quality, never cheap-grade, primer.
- Use good-quality paint.
- Apply thin coats, just enough to cover.

Removing Old Paint

To this date, no one has invented an easy way to remove old paint. One of the easiest methods, for a house in really bad condition, is to use a pressure washer, which is a very high-pressure water hose. This equipment can be rented from a tool rental place. Even from the ground, you easily can get about as much off as you can by hand scraping; if you get up close to the work, the pressure will take a lot off.

Under certain circumstances, heat, in the form of a butane torch or a blow torch, can be used to get off old paint. You will use a great deal of fuel if you use butane. There is a very large stipulation attached to this method: *Never, never use fire to strip anything attached to the walls of the house.* This includes siding, eaves, window trim, hollow porch posts, and porch roof structure. An updraft through a crack may carry the flame right up the cavity of the wall and you will have a three-alarm fire as quickly as you can say "fire sale." In addition, do not use heat to remove lead-based paint—and, in all likelihood, your old house will have lead paint.

Electric paint strippers, which burn paint off without a flame, are now available. They work very well and are much safer than using a torch.

The time-honored method is to scrape. You must settle beforehand that successful scraping comes only with your willingness to scrape, sweat, and ache. So, keep your paint scrapers sharp and scrape away! Get off all the loose stuff that will come with reasonable effort. You can't take too much off, as long as your patience doesn't fail you. Supply yourself with extra blades so you can keep a sharp blade in your scraper without frequent trips to the shop for sharpening, or at least take a good file up on the ladder with you and sharpen the blade as you go. Though scraping paint is a miserable job, often taking more time than the painting itself, don't neglect it. The longevity of your paint job will be determined largely by the thoroughness of your scraping job.

Caulking and Priming

Caulk all cracks with a good quality latex or silicone caulk. Latex is much easier to handle, but silicone is longer lasting and is especially good in cracks where nothing else will stay. For more routine caulking, use latex caulk. It is half the cost and readily washes off your hands.

As important as scraping is, it is equally critical to prime all bare wood, new or old, with a good quality primer. If you don't prime the bare wood, the paint will peel in record time! In some cases, there is so much bare wood showing after you have scraped the house that it is best to cover the whole wall with primer, giving special attention to the bare spots. If you are going to paint your house a dark color, consider tinting the primer. This makes it easier to cover the primer with the first coat of paint.

Window Sills

Window sills and other horizontal wood surfaces are often badly deteriorated. Small weather-cracks can be filled with a good-quality caulk or a filler especially formulated for patching rotten sills. Thereafter, carefully maintain with paint. I recommend the very best silicone caulk for this job, but, check the label to see if it can be painted—some can and some can't.

If the sills are badly deteriorated and rotted, they probably are hopeless, and you will need to whittle them out and replace them. Be sure to use treated lumber for the replacement sills.

The best flashing material for patches is a fairly heavy grade of primed aluminum flashing. It handles well and will take paint so that your patches will be inconspicuous at close range and invisible at 10 or 15 feet. They will last indefinitely.

Siding

Existing siding may need repair in some areas of the house. You can
- Replace with boards that match the present siding
- Replace with hardboard siding (never use vinyl, aluminum, or cheap-grade wooden siding)
- Cover bad spots with small patches of flashing material nailed on with 3d box nails

Choosing Your Paint

Paint your house with a good-quality paint if you are going to paint it at all. With the great amount of labor involved, you certainly do not want to use a paint that will not stick. On the whole, I feel that a *better* grade (not necessarily the costly top-of-the-line variety) of any name-brand paint is sufficient. In paint, you get what you pay for. Look for sales or discounts to save money, but know the brand you select. Avoid the cheapest grades because you will just have to put on more coats to get good coverage.

Oil or Latex?

The war goes on about whether oil- or latex-based paints are better. Some—and these generally include professional painters—insist that oil-based paint permeates the surface of the wood better. A lot of the prejudice against latex paint remains from its flaws of some years back. The thing that makes it so desirable is that clean-up is much easier than with oil. When you paint for short

---

Do not put oil-based paint over latex. Once you start using latex, continue to use it.

---

periods of time, this makes a great deal of difference. Furthermore, when working with latex, you can paint when the weather is damp, even in a rainstorm, as long as you are working in a spot where the rain cannot wash off the wet paint and the wood you are painting isn't saturated. I am convinced that latex paint is basically the paint of the future, with one exception: I often use oil-based primer when covering old, bare wood.

Colors

Many old houses respond wonderfully to a widely varied color scheme. Late nineteenth-century houses come alive when all the elaborate decoration for which they are known is highlighted. Three, four, or even five colors are not unreasonable on some houses, often making an unbelievable difference to a house that was once thought to be quite plain.

Generally, the wise approach is to paint the body of the house a lighter color (usually not white) and the framing boards, windows, shutters, moldings, and decorations darker colors. Here is a place to let your imagination soar. I have seen colors that were, in my mind's eye, an outrageous combination but, tried on a particular house, they have been very beautiful.

English Tudor-style houses usually look best if painted within a very restricted color range, with the exposed beams a dark color, and the plaster, white, cream, or gray.

If you don't trust your color sense, ask someone who does. I have seen old houses that were changed as much as day from night, merely by the selection of the right colors. Choose wisely.

Ways to Make the Job Seem Easier

One way of lessening the burden of house painting is to paint your house continuously by doing a side every year or so. Such a maintenance program allows you to spread out the cost of the paint, and perhaps even better, it enables you to face what might, otherwise, seem an insurmountable task. The disadvantage in painting a house this way is that you pretty much have to stick with the same color scheme, unless you don't mind having different colors on different sides of the house for a time.

If you are compelled by the urgency of your need for paint, or by your own tidy personal preference to paint your house all at once, don't try to do *all* of each step before moving on to the next one. For example,

1. Scrape for a half a day.
2. Prime what is scraped.
3. Next day, paint the primed work of the preceding day before beginning to scrape again.

In this manner, you will encourage yourself by the bright, clean results of each day's work and gain the added benefit of not having to move your ladders so many times.

Tips for Painting with a Brush

- Mix paint well, especially oil paint.
- Punch three small holes in the seal rim of your paint can to allow paint to drain into the pail.
- Use as wide a brush as the strength in your arm and hand will permit.
- Keep a 1- or 1 1/4-inch sash brush, free from frayed ends, for painting next to glass or change-of-color lines. Draw the line in a long sweep instead of little daubing motions.

- Transfer paint to a bucket larger than your brush is wide by 2 inches. (You will ruin the outer edges of a 4-inch brush catching them on the edge of a standard paint can.)
- Dip only the tip in the paint; keep paint out of the ferrule area of the brush.
- Wipe the loaded brush on the side of the pail so paint will not drip on the ground or run into the ferrule on overhead painting.
- Brush with long sweeping, not poking, motions.

To keep your brushes in good condition and avoid mess, the paint can opening should be at least 2 inches larger than the width of the paint brush; dip only the tip of the brush into the paint.

Spray Painting

Spray painting has a bad reputation, I believe, for several unfortunate reasons:

- People too lazy to brush are too lazy to scrape; *how* the finish coat is applied is irrelevant if the surface has been inadequately prepared.
- People looking for a cheap way to get a paint job use cheap paint and do not prime.
- Too thin a coat is applied (although often, sprayed-on paint sticks better in the long run than brushed-on paint *because* of thinner coats).

Spraying may be particularly suited to special problems you

have on your house. These problems might include such things as
- Shingles
- Louvered shutters
- Rough-sawn wood
- Extensive and intricate decoration
- Large amount of porch balustrades and other gingerbread

Painting with Rollers

Some outside painting, such as the following, can be done with a roller with an extension handle:
- Priming bare spots
- Trim that is hard to reach with a brush
- Porch ceilings
- Porch floors and steps
- Shingled exteriors

Rollers do not give good coverage on the lower lip of clapboards, because your position on the ground requires that you roll up and down rather than side to side. Nevertheless, there might be an otherwise inaccessible area where rolling on paint is just the ticket.

Shutters, Windows, Doors, and Porches

Shutters

Old buildings often have shutters on them. If you are lacking enough shutters to go with every window, compromise by at least shuttering all the windows on the front of the house or all those on the ground floor. In the South, shutters were used originally to shade out sun or to protect against storms. These were hung on shutter hinges and had hooks to hold them open. Such an arrangement precludes the use of screens, unless they are interior screens, which slide up and down on tracks inside the window sash so as not to hinder the closing of the shutters.

With vertical adjustment rod
facing out, screw shutters
securely in place so that they
overlap the side window casings.

Tips on Hanging Shutters

- Hang shutters so that they cover the side window casings, the vertical adjustment rod faces the viewer.
- If you do not have shutter hinges, screw the shutters onto the casings. (Pulling nails each time you paint would destroy the shutters.)
- If the shutters are not original to the window and are too short, add a strip to the top to make them as high as the window opening.
- If the shutters are not original to the window and are too long, cut them off just under the top crosspiece, remove as many slats and as much of the sides as necessary to match the size of the window opening, and then replace the top crosspiece. (See illustration.)
- If the shutter sags, strengthen it with a wire secured diagonally across the back.
- Screw metal strips on the shutter back to fasten loose joints.

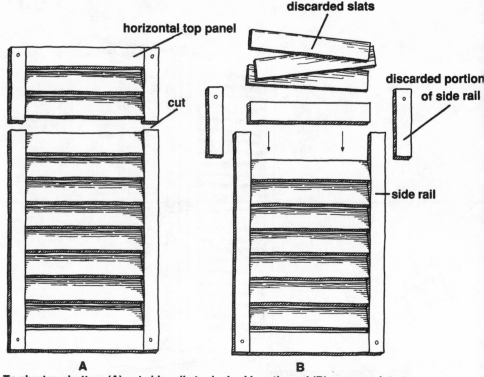

To shorten shutters (A) cut side rails to desired length, and (B) remove slats to make room for the horizontal top panel; slip top panel into place and fasten to the side rails with pegs or metal corner brackets.

Windows

As I said earlier (see pages 78-79), storm windows both protect existing windows and prevent heat loss through windows that don't fit very well any more. If you use storm windows, you will save yourself from a life sentence of window glazing, but you will probably have to glaze some (maybe all) windows at the outset. A window with loose glass in it lets a lot of heat out of your house. A storm window over a window that needs glazing is just about as effective as a well-glazed window with no storm. You might just as well glaze the windows and save the price of storm windows if that's all the energy savings—and comfort—you care about. In addition, a loose glass is much more likely to break than a secure one.

How to Glaze Windows
the Old-Fashioned Way

1. If the glass is not well secured in the sash, you must put more

glazing points in the sash to hold the glass firmly. Formerly, glazing points were little triangular objects that only a magician or a brain surgeon could get into the wood. Now, push points have a little ledge against which you can easily push them in with your glazing knife.

2. Clean away all old, loose putty. If the old putty on the sash is firm, you need not replace it. Very hard putty that needs to come out can be loosened with a butane torch. If you try to chip it out with a chisel you will very likely break the glass.

3. Use a very stiff putty knife or glazing knife (which is like a putty knife with a 40° bend in the blade) and a good, name-brand glazing compound. Be sure the glazing compound is fresh and moist. (Never buy it in large cans because it will dry out before you use it all.)

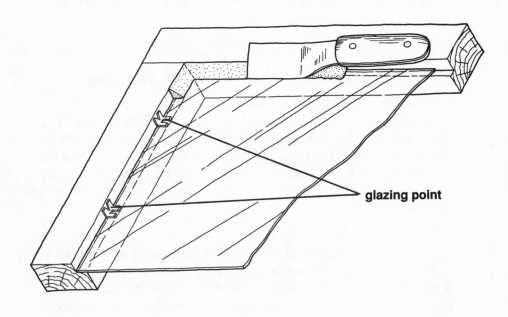

glazing point

Hold putty knife at an angle a bit flatter than 45°, and press harder on the back side of the knife than on the forward side when pushing glazing compound into the area in one smooth operation.

4. Clean the glass and sash well.
5. Prime wooden parts and allow to dry thoroughly.
6. Place a glob of glazing compound near a corner of the pane. You will discover by experience how much glazing compound you will need for various-sized panes.
7. Hold the putty knife at an angle a little bit flatter than 45°.
8. Push against the glazing compound very hard, moving it the whole length of the area to be glazed in one operation and pressing harder on the back side of the knife, with less pressure on the forward side of the knife. If the glazing compound rolls out of the space reserved for it, the surface is dirty, you are not pushing down hard enough, or, the glazing compound has gotten too stiff.
9. To assure a long-lasting job, paint the surface of the glazing compound after it is in place. I have heard of people mixing paint with the glazing compound before glazing the window, but to me that seems like a good way to have an exceptionally messy job.

The Lazy Person's Alternative to Glazing Windows the Old-Fashioned Way

Glazing is now sold in tubes that can be used with a caulking gun. Even with this simplified method, you must begin with a clean and dry window. Use a steady hand to apply the glazing. Smooth out rough spots with a putty knife after the glazing has dried a little.

Cracked Window Glass

Some people replace all cracked glass whether there is a piece missing or not, although actually, a crack does not let out a great deal of heat. But if anyone slams shut a window that has cracked glass, it will break much more easily than one that is not cracked. Many people so prize the old wavy glass that they are unwilling to replace it with new glass even when it has a crack. Personally, I am too lazy and too poor to replace glass that is merely cracked. If it *is* just cracked and not displaced, you can seal it with a drop of strong adhesive such as Superglue. Capillary action should pull the thin liquid along the crack. In many cases the crack will almost disappear.

Tips on Protecting Stained Glass

Stained or leaded glass might need a custom-made storm window both to prevent cold coming in through the lead joints and to protect the lead. Alternatively, you could fit a piece of 1/4-inch plexiglass or plate glass over the whole window, and secure it with glazing. Do not glaze it in with such permanence that you can never get it out. In ten or fifteen years you can get a build-up of grease and dirt between the windows even when they seem to be sealed.

Be sure that the metal bars that hold the leaded glass in place are in good condition and still soldered to the lead.

Doors

Badly deteriorated, sagging, or warped doors are not only unsightly but they are irritating to use and sources of energy loss. A variety of problems require a variety of solutions.

Possible Problems with Old Doors

Problem	Solution
Poor fit	Install weather stripping.
	Put a thicker molding, called a *door stop*, around the door frame.
Loose hinge screws	Use slightly longer screws.
	Put glue on a toothpick, insert the toothpick into the screwhole and break it off flush with the surface. Immediately drive the

screw into the hole.

Pulling apart at the two top seams	First, pull the seams together tightly. A pipe clamp, which consists of two jaws made to fit around a half-inch pipe, makes this job easier. Then make the seam fast by one of the following methods:

Nail a piece of screen molding across the door at the top on both front and back

or

Drill a hole through the side edge into the top rail and gently drive a glue-covered dowel into the hole

or

Drill a pilot hole through the side edge into the top rail for a lag screw; the hole should be the size of the shaft in the middle of the screw's threads.
Drill a second, shorter hole to accommodate the lag screw shank.
Countersink the head of the lag screw.

Warped door	Use clamps and shims to bow the door back slightly *past* straight. Glue and nail a 2-inch wide strip of 1/4-inch plywood down the whole length of the vertical panel of the door on the side where the tension is required (usually the outside). Let it dry overnight, then remove the clamps. If the door stays straight, fit strips the rest of the way around the door to make the strip look intentional.

Maybe no remedy other than to make the door stop crooked enough to meet the door in its warped condition.

Consider trading the warped door for a similar door, in good condition, from elsewhere in the house where it is less important to have a good fit.

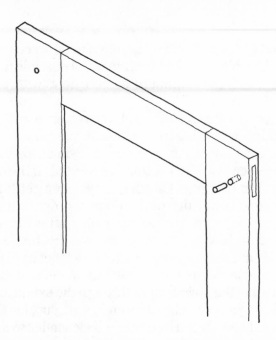

To repair two separating top seams of a door, pull the parts together and hold them in place with a pipe clamp, then drill a pilot hole through the side edge into the top rail and gently drive a glue-covered dowel into the hole.

Glass Doors

If you need to replace glass in doors, you must follow a slightly different procedure than you use for windows. Glass that is set in doors is usually secured by wooden molding, tacked with the smallest wire brads possible to avoid splitting the moldings and also to make removal easy. This molding makes points unnecessary. In addition to these moldings, the glass is set in a thin coat of glazing compound, both to keep the cold out and to prevent the glass from rattling or breaking when the door is slammed. If your door originally contained beveled glass that has been broken, you should probably replace it with plain double-strength glass. Unfortunately, beveled glass costs a king's ransom, unless you can swap something from your treasure room for glass from another collector's stock.

Screen Doors

Often it is hard to know what to do about screen doors in old houses. It is unlikely that the house's antique screen doors will have withstood all that banging! Yet old houses, which generally are not equipped with air conditioning, often need screen doors in order to be comfortable, and I feel that the worst possible thing you could do is to install an aluminum screen door with a bright aluminum panel at the bottom.

I have had considerable success, however, in using a stock wooden screen door and fixing it up to look like an old screen door. If the new door is smaller than the opening, add strips the same thickness as the door to top and bottom, as needed. If the opening is much bigger than the largest stock door you can get (usually 3 feet), add a piece to both sides of the door in order to make the width of the two sides of the door equal. Fasten these strip additions with dowels whether they are on the hinge or the slamming side, because they are going to get a lot of hard use. To attach the strips, glue them in place, tack them on, and then drill holes the diameter of the dowels right through the extension piece into the door. Load your dowels with waterproof glue, tap them in, and cut them off. Sand the surface with a disk sander to level the door and the extension and then with a vibrator sander for a fine finish.

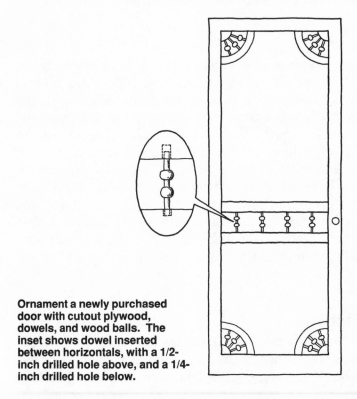

Ornament a newly purchased door with cutout plywood, dowels, and wood balls. The inset shows dowel inserted between horizontals, with a 1/2-inch drilled hole above, and a 1/4-inch drilled hole below.

Most of these doors have a double crosspiece at the middle. Here is the place to insert 3/4-inch balls glued on dowels. You can get the balls, already drilled with 1/4-inch holes, in any craft store. Make your own design, but the most common nineteenth-century design was two balls on a dowel, with the dowels spaced about every 2 inches across the door. The way I get the dowels into the space between the crosspieces is to drill exactly 1/4 inch into the lower one and at least 1/2 inch into the upper one at the proper location for the dowels. Then I make my dowels 1/2 inch longer than the space between the crosspieces. Having done this, it is easy to poke the dowel up into the upper hole and then down into the lower hole and set it with glue and a tiny brad.

In one, two, or all corners of the screen openings make corner decorations. Cut out a quarter of a rim of a wheel from waterproof plywood and use dowels, fitted with balls, to make three or four spokes. Alternative corner decorations might be stylized bat wings or smaller and finer versions of the corner brackets used for the porch openings. Finally, stain the whole door with a dark stain and apply several coats of waterproof varnish. You also could paint it, but the contrasting touch of natural wood against all the other painted surfaces is quite handsome.

Porches

The most needy areas on the exterior of many houses are the porches. Exposed as they are to the elements, their horizontal parts catch both rain and snow. Good maintenance includes
- Repairing leaky roofs
- Clearing clogged gutters
- Painting frequently

If these things have been neglected, you very likely will have some or many of the problems that follow.

A Baker's Dozen Porch Diseases and Their Cures

If the *understructure is rotten*, you may be in for a complete rebuilding job. For this or any other porch work, if you must buy new wood, spend the extra dollars to get treated lumber. Whether you use new or secondhand lumber, however, make sure you stop the source of the water that damaged the porch in the first place.

In some cases there are alternatives to a complete rebuilding job.
- Double damaged joists.
- Replace a rotted place in the sill with a concrete block or brick, as long as the weak spot is not structural or visible.
- For a year or so, until you can fix it permanently, set an extra 4x4-post on a brick.

If the *floor is rotten*, you may have to replace it. But if there are only a few bad spots, and they are still firm enough, you might buy some time by putting in temporary sheet-metal patches over the rotting places in the floor. Nail these down with 3d or 4d coated box nails; caulk the edges and paint to match. You may also be able to replace sections of floor only. However, no fair cutting off, say, the last two feet of all the boards along the edge of the porch and replacing them. Rain will run in the new seam and further destroy the floor; then you'll have both the floor *and* the understructure to fix.

The problem of a few *missing balusters* can be disguised by removing all balusters, then respacing them to fill the balustrade evenly. If nearly all balusters are gone, you will have to replace them with square ones cut out of 1 1/8-inch stock. You can also cut decorative balusters from plywood using a borrowed design. Or, turnings can be purchased fairly reasonably from mail-order supply houses. Often, a low porch can go without a balustrade.

Balusters often rot at the bottom where the water settles. To repair this problem, cut about 3/4-inch off the bottom of each and raise the lower balustrade to accommodate the new length of the

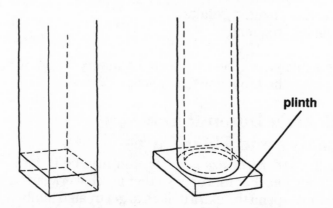

(A) A newly cut block replaces rotted-out portion of square post. (B) A square "plinth" replaces rotted-out portion of hollow round post.

balusters.

Solid, turned or square *porch posts often rot at the bottom.* To repair,

1. Cut rotted part of post off.
2. Cut a block of the same dimension to replace the cut-off portion. If you want a round block, have one cut with a band saw.
3. Caulk and sand the joint well.
4. If the post is square, add a baseboard around the bottom to camouflage the addition.
5. To repair hollow round or square posts, cut off 2 to 4 inches of damaged wood and compensate for the shortened length by adding an extra plinth at the bottom and/or an extra capital at the top. Caulk and sand well before painting.

If you keep a metal porch roof in good condition by frequently painting it with a good roof paint and never allowing rotting leaves to lie on it, it will last for the life of the house.

If your roof is a *deteriorated tin roof,* try replacing it with double-lap, roll roofing. On steep roofs, where the roof is clearly visible, use shingles or 5v metal roofing. If you absolutely cannot get permanent repairs done immediately but are (justifiably) concerned about continued deterioration that will damage the floor and other parts of the porch structure, lay a polyethylene tarp on the roof and glue it down with roofing cement or, for short term, weight it down with bricks. Patch *scattered leaks* with fiberized roofing cement or pieces of roofing or flashing material glued in with generous gobs of roofing cement. *For small leaks and obviously deteriorated metal roofing,* paint the whole roof with roofing tar. For best results, the roof must be dry and hot.

For self-cleaning gutters, *instead of using downspouts, simply leave one end of the gutter open and allow it to protrude 6 inches from the end of the roof. A heavy downpour will clean all the leaves out automatically. This method may cause drainage problems of its own, however. Be sure that water does not flow back in under the porch or house foundation. To avoid erosion at the point where the water falls, lay down a circle of stones or gravel.*

Leaky built-in gutters can sometimes be fixed by adding patches in the same manner as described above for adding patches to metal roofs. If there are many leaks, cover the gutters first with plywood, then with roofing material. Install add-on gutters.

Porches need gutters more than any other place on the house, because without them, the wind will blow the drip all over the porch. *Stopped-up gutters*, however, are a semiannual plague, ten times as bad as no gutters at all. If they are not cleaned, they will overflow, carrying rain just where you don't want it, to rot and stain your porch beyond belief. Further, the gutters themselves will soon rot and need replacement.

Inadequate pitch of the porch floor is likely a construction mistake. To correct this problem, you must get to the understructure and lower the outside edge just enough so the water flows off. If you find a dip in the surface where the water settles, jack up the low place by putting a 4x4 "leg" under it.

Porch flooring has a peculiar but often unknown characteristic. Every board contains a warp, which forms a little concave trough that directs the water to the edge of the porch and prevents it from running sideways and into the cracks. This warping to provide a concave surface was assured by old-time carpenters by the way they selected the grain. Modern porch flooring is scored on the back side of the board to guarantee that it will warp correctly. If you do not use new porch flooring, be sure to observe the grain of the flooring and lay the boards with the concave surface face up.

A *porch that slopes too much* usually signals problems in the support structure underneath—rotten pilings or sinking brick piers. Sometimes the porch slopes so precariously, one can imagine all the furniture and people sitting on it sliding off.

The first step in solving the problem is to improve drainage so that water no longer can get in around the porch supports. With a dry foundation assured, replace all rotted wooden posts. Brick piers probably don't need to be removed if you add shims when the porch is raised up to a proper level. A hydraulic automobile jack is usually strong enough to lift the porch. The bigger the tonnage of the jack, the better. You will know it is in its correct position when the balustrade is level, the posts are plumb, and the opening formed by the balustrade, the cornice, and the posts is square. In

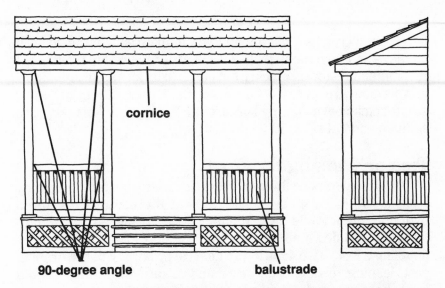

cornice

90-degree angle   **balustrade**

(A) A porch is in the correct position when the balustrade is level, the posts are plumb, and the opening formed by the balustrade, cornice, and posts is square. (B) The porch floor alone should slope slightly away from the house.

other words, only the floor should slope, not the whole porch. (See illustration.)

Missing gingerbread, such as the small, turned balusters at the top of the porch opening or some forms of ball-on-dowel decoration, are often irreplaceable. You can sometimes cut your own decoration from 5/8- or 3/4-inch waterproof plywood, using an authentic design from another house of the age and style of yours.

Modernized porches are a different problem. You may find, for example, that a former owner has poured a concrete floor for the porch. Because porch floors made of concrete were standard on new houses built after 1920, porches needing repair on older houses often received the same treatment. These certainly are beautiful and maintenance-free floors. When the work was done as a repair, the porch area was usually filled with dirt, over which the concrete was poured. Occasionally, you will find one where the concrete was poured right over the floor boards. You may just have to live with such a modernization.

If, on the other hand, someone has added a solid, plywood- or shingle-covered balustrade, you will do well to remove it and make a new balustrade, consistent with the age and character of your house.

Perhaps no other aspect of the modernization of an old house ruins a house so absolutely as an enclosed porch. Further, such a porch often creates a dilemma: Even if unattractive, the space it provides is convenient to have. If at all possible, however, I recommend restoring an old front porch to its former usage. Boost up your courage, take a deep breath, think happy thoughts—and swing a pickax or a digging bar through the front wall of that porch addition and get rid of it!

Tips on Raising the Roof

If you need to raise the porch roof to take the posts out for some reason, you can usually jack it up with the use of 4x4s and a hydraulic automobile jack, mounted on a plank so the weight doesn't press down all in one place. The 4x4s can be made by doubling a 2x4. Two 4x4s in the general proximity of the original post, leaning toward each other and toward the house should easily hold the roof up while you take the post out.

If the porch roof is not too heavy, you should be able to lift it high enough to replace posts or flooring by following this procedure:
- Place one end of a 4x4 under a convenient lifting place. The other end should rest on the ground about one foot out from where it would be if it were straight up and down.
- Put a solid heavy plank under the ground end. With the biggest sledge hammer you can find, drive the 4x4 into a vertical position.

Posts, Railings, and Decorative Trim

Train your eye to the appropriateness of trim for different styles of architecture when you must replace missing elements. If you have to improvise,
- Replace hard-to-find turned posts or hollow, round posts, with 4x4 posts or square, hollow posts respectively; they are cheap and easy to make.
- Replace missing or rotted railings with 2x4s or 2x6s; taper the upper surface to each side of a centerline.
- Use a jigsaw to cut your own gingerbread from 3/4- or 5/8-inch sanded plywood; it is cheaper and actually better lasting than the solid boards used in the past.

Other Tips to Save Time and Money on Porches
- Always keep your porch floor painted and it will never rot. Paint that is worn down to the wood is a sign that you need to

roll a new coat of paint on it.

- Give your porch floor only one coat of paint the first year. Add a second coat after one year and a third coat after two years.
- Instead of using a brush, roll paint on porch ceilings with a long-napped, fluffy roller cover. You'll save time and mess.
- If your porch posts and balusters have so much paint on them that it cracks and chips off before the rest of your house needs painting, touch up the bare spots with primer. If you tint the primer to match the finish-coat house paint, you may be able to avoid a final coat until your next serious paint job.
- Keep saucers under your hanging porch plants, or hang plants from the outer edge of the eaves, so that they do not drip water onto your balustrade and floor, causing rot, peeling paint, and mildew.
- Keep wet and rotting leaves out of your gutters and off of your metal porch roof.
- Plant foundation shrubbery considerably away from porch so that even when the plantings grow you can walk behind them. Close shrubbery causes splatter and dampness, both of which rot porches.
- Keep the underside of your porch enclosed. You don't want cats and dogs and other freeloaders to live and play there. Enclosure also gives your house a better, more finished appearance. If the porch crawl space does not connect with the rest of the basement, use lattice, which looks great and is quite cheap. Otherwise, use bricks or waterproof plywood. For brick or plywood enclosures, be sure to leave some vent space, preferably screened.

Chimneys and Roofs

Chimneys

Even if you don't plan to use a stove or fireplace with your chimney, you may still need it, for not only may the central heating system or the gas hot-water heater be vented out the chimney, but a chimney is often a part of your house's beauty. Even though as a functional chimney it is worthless, it may be an integral part of the house, and thus ought not to be removed. Because chimneys are freestanding and thus exposed to the frost at night and the heat of the sun in the afternoon, chimneys are prone to many disorders, however, including loose mortar, missing bricks, or, often, a lean, usually to the east or north, whichever way the broad dimension of the chimney is oriented.

The best remedy for a deteriorated chimney is to disassemble it, brick by brick, down to the roof and start over again with the same bricks and new mortar. You will have to build a scaffold around the chimney big enough to hold all the bricks that you remove. Try to get a helper on the ground to send you up tools and mortar in a bucket attached to a rope. This is a back-breaking job—and not for anyone who fears heights—but it can be done. Look at old chimneys of the right period for examples to follow and you might even improve on its original beauty. If you put a chimney tile into the new chimney, it will probably make your job last longer than the original did.

Flash the chimney where it adjoins the roof, going from the lowest point, up-roof.

Making Old Chimneys Safe

The rest of the chimney, from the roof on down to the basement, may not be much better than the part that sticks up. Peering down it with a powerful flashlight on an overcast day may give you some idea of its condition. You should examine your chimney thoroughly, particularly if you have a wood furnace, woodstove, or a working fireplace. If your chimney has a tile-lined flue, then you are probably safe in using it. If the chimney is unlined, the slightest hole in the mortar may produce a draft that will cause the flames from an overheated fireplace to go out through the hole and burn your house like an over-roasted marshmallow on a skewer.

Every appliance, such as an oil burner, a gas burner, and a woodstove, must have a separate flue.

It is possible to line old chimneys with stainless steel chimney liner. This job is best done by professionals. Some installers pour a special cement between the liner and the masonry, for additional protection. Be certain that the juncture of the stovepipe and the top of the stove or fireplace is securely sealed so that all the smoke and heat goes up the pipe, otherwise, some of the flame could go up the outside of the pipe, seek a draft through a gap in the mortar, and start a fire.

If you get professionals to reline your chimney, I recommend obtaining a guarantee from them so that if the liner isn't solid and a fire results, you have legal recourse. For further information on safe chimney installations, obtain a recent code book from the National Fire Protection Association (available from chimney and stove suppliers and installers) and inquire about local codes at your fire department.

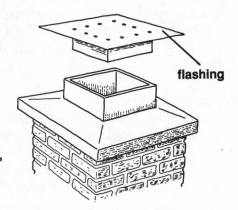

flashing

When box is plugged into chimney, bend overlapping flashing slightly downward over the outside of the chimney.

How to Cap a Chimney

Unused chimneys can be capped with tin or aluminum flashing material

- To keep birds, beasts, and leaves out
- To prevent water damage caused by rain running down to the bottom
- To preserve the life of the chimney

Don't try to nail the flashing to the chimney, as this may break the mortar and weaken the chimney. Make a wooden box about one inch smaller than the hole. Nail a piece of tin slightly larger than the chimney to the box. Plug the box into the chimney like a wine cork into a bottle. Bend the overhanging edges slightly downward over the outside of the chimney.

The Roof

Putting on a new roof can seem a formidable project to a person who has never laid a roof before. The first decision that faces you is whether, indeed, you really *need* a new roof. You do *not* need a new roof just because

- You have a leak here and there: You may need only to find and stop the leaks

- A dozen shingles blew off: You may need only to replace a dozen shingles
- Leaks occur around a chimney or a dormer: You may need only to improve or replace the flashing
- You need a roof on an addition: You may need only to roof the worn section. Roll roofing (roofing material available in a long, rolled sheet rather than bundles of shingles) wears out more quickly than shingles, and roofing on a flatter roof often wears out more quickly than roofing on the steep, main roof of the house. South-facing roofs wear out faster than north-facing roofs.

You *do* need a new roof if
- Roofing is so brittle that you can't slide patches under it
- Valleys in the roof have worn through and are leaking
- Huge sections of the roof have blown off, making a new roof a more sensible investment than tedious patching efforts
- Repeated new leaks appear after old ones are stopped

If all this overwhelms you, don't be afraid to call on a roofing salesperson, even if you plan to do your own roofing. At least, you will know how much you are saving by doing the work yourself. At most, you may discover that the savings are not worth the trouble of doing your own work.

If a roofing salesperson tries to convince you against your better judgment that you need a new roof, take the advice with a grain of salt, and always get a second opinion—if possible, from someone who doesn't stand to make a profit.

Patching Old Roofs

There are two solutions to most things having to do with roof leaks. One of them is the substance called *roofing tar, or coating*, a brush-on tar that really seals up a roof. It is available plain or mixed with aluminum paint. It is especially valuable for painting over leaky joints in roll roofing or over all nailheads in a section where you suspect that you have a leak around one nailhead in a hundred and don't have a ghost of an idea which one it is. Roofing tar goes on best when the roof is so hot you can't stand to work on it, although it will work almost as well when it is a little cooler than that. If you are forced to put it on in cool weather, try getting the tar warmed up to 90°F. before you spread it. Be careful in heating it though: If it ever gets so hot that it catches fire, you'll never put the fire out.

The other solution to a leaky roof is *roofing cement*, a fiber-filled compound intended to fill up holes and patch damaged places. It does not last forever but will do a marvelous job on many different kinds of leaks for a good number of years.

Both of these products have a mysterious quality that causes them to jump out and attach themselves to your clothes when you seemingly have not even been near the can. And experience shows that the better condition your clothes are in, the more easily they can jump out of the can and affix themselves to you. Wear old clothes and shoes when doing any sort of roofing patch.

Finding the Leak

Look for suspicious nailheads, missing shingles, or flashing at the spot just above the leak.

Examine the area all the way up the roof from the leak to the ridge. Leaks often run down a rafter before they decide to let go and drop in the most inconvenient spot in the room—on your bed, in your closet, or on an antique velvet chair. Tar anything that looks suspicious and wait for the next rainstorm. Don't let failure stop you from trying one more time. Often it will take three or four tries before you find the right spot.

Tips on Fixing Leaks

- If you have missing shingles on the roof, glue some new ones on with roofing cement.
- Use roofing cement or tin flashing around chimneys and dormers where water is leaking in.
- Slate and metal roofs in their sunset years can often be nursed along by covering them with a coat of roofing tar at the first sign of trouble. It might be three or four years before they begin to leak once more, allowing you the chance to put off a big roofing job (and bill) for a bit longer.
- Tile roofs can be repaired with roofing cement, but regular mortar is longer-lasting.
- When a tin or tile roof over an attic leaks only when a driving wind blows rain in, you may get by with putting plastic buckets or sheeting in the attic under the leak. Any collected water will evaporate before the next bad storm.

New Roofing: Shingles

It may be that you cannot talk your way out of it and you are faced with the stark reality of putting on a new roof. The difficulty lies more in the sheer size of the project than in its demand for any particular skills. Let's take it step-by-step.

First, you must determine whether or not you have a solid deck under the roof. Sometimes you may find a wood shingle roof laid on lath down under many subsequent layers of roofing. If this is the case, you have three alternatives, in order from easiest, to best and most expensive:

1. Leave all roofing in place and lay your new shingles with nails long enough to go through all the layers into the boards.
2. Remove all roofing material, including the original wooden shingles, and then cut boards to fit in the openings between the slats. This is especially sensible if you have access to low- or no-cost, secondhand boards. Use boards that are approximately the right size, and cut them in with a sharp carpenter's axe. Work from the ridge down, so that you can stand in the spaces between the boards as if they were steps of a ladder.
3. Remove all roofing material, including the original wooden shingles but not the lath, sheathe with plywood, and then lay a new roof over it as if you were roofing a new house. Although 1/2-inch plywood is sufficient, 5/8-inch is better. Sometimes particle board is used, but it is not very strong and it is very heavy and hard to handle, especially at roof height.

Warning: When you remove layers of roofing, watch your step! *One rotted spot and you can easily fall right through.*

Tips for an Easier Roofing Job

- Obtain several ladders, so that you aren't constantly moving a ladder. Better still, rent scaffolding or a power lift. A lift is helpful for getting all those shingles up to the roof.
- Use a square, pointed shovel or an old-fashioned ice scraper to remove old shingles.
- Rent or borrow an open trailer to park under the eaves to catch the trash. Picking up old shingles and other debris is almost as much work as stripping the roof in the first place.
- Cover the open roof with polyethylene plastic before you quit

for the day; an unexpected heavy rain could ruin all of the ceilings in the house if you don't. Once the surface is ready for roofing, it can be protected for a week or two with tarpaper, stapled to the bare wood.

- The best roofs are laid in hot weather—hot enough to sit on the roof but not so hot (and soft) that it burns you or is easily marked as you stand on it.
- In cold weather leave 3/16-inch spaces between each strip of shingle. If you don't, they will expand and buckle when they heat up.
- The traditional method for scaffolding is to tie a 2x4 to a wire (of the kind shingles are bundled with) and nail it to the roof for a toe-hold. Shingles are laid over the wire with the 2x4 on top of the finished roof below. When the toe-hold needs to be moved up the roof, the wire is simply cut just above the edge of the shingle from which it protrudes. It is much easier—and safer—however, to buy or rent a set of roof jacks.
- Give careful attention to starting the shingles on the horizontal chalk lines. Many roofers stagger the slots because perfectly straight rows of slots tend to channel the water and erode more quickly. If you do line them up, however, they must be straight along the vertical as well as the horizontal chalk line, so that all the "cut-outs" of the shingles line up as you look up the roof from the ground.
- The best way to cut the shingle ends is score the back side of the shingle with a *box cutter*, then bend it so that it breaks on the score.
- Flash all chimneys and dormers as you go.
- Use heavy roofing or flashing material for the valleys, which get special wear.

Alternative Roofing Materials:
Barn Tin and Roll Roofing

Another kind of roofing that is frequently used today, is *barn tin*, sometimes called 5v or 7v roofing. It is available with both galvanized and aluminum finishes, as well as more expensive colored varieties. You can save that cost by using the galvanized or aluminum version, letting it weather for about a year, and then painting it. Many of the older roofs were made of *tern metal* (tin-plated steel, from which the term *tin roof* comes). Although it looked somewhat like barn tin, it was soldered in place and marvelously waterproof. Standing-seam, tin-plate roofing is still available and is one of the best roofs you can buy. You can use 5v barn tin on a house roof as long as you are sure that every nail is snugly into the wood and all mistakes are filled with a squirt of silicone sealing compound. Formerly barn-tin roofs were fastened down with lead nails, but now nails with neoprene washers are used. I recommend adding a polyethylene plastic liner to keep small leaks in joints from causing trouble during driving rainstorms.

Flat-roofed additions might be covered with *double-lap roll roofing*, such as is used on porch roofs (see page 99). Double-lap roll roofing is an improvement over the old roll roofing because no nails show and there are at least two layers of roofing over the entire surface.

Ornamentation on Porches

In houses built anytime from the 1830s through the end of the nineteenth century, the peak of the gable was often decorated with patterns sawed out of wood or with a combination of cutouts, turnings, and balls. These decorations may or may not have matched the motif of the porch gingerbread. Houses built in the 1920s often featured heavy brackets along the cornices under the eaves or balustrades on the porch roof. Many old houses are missing their distinctive decoration, however, and will be greatly enhanced if your loving care returns some of their earlier ornament. Beware, however, that you do choose appropriately. Highly decorated nineteenth-century houses appear in a bewildering array of styles—Gothic Revival, Italian Villa, Second Empire, Eastlake, Stick, Queen Anne, and Shingle are among the most popular (see pages 111-12). Cut-out or turned wooden decorations are quite suitable for some of these, but be guided by the surviving ornament on your house or on other similar houses in your neighborhood. Late nineteenth-century ornamentation on a Federal period house, a colonial New England weathervane on a mid-nineteenth-century Italian villa, or Pennsylvania Dutch decoration on a Greek Revival house are all equally offensive. If style is confusing to you—and it *is* a complex subject—talk to preservationists and restoration experts, get some style books out of the library, visit as many old houses as you can, and soon you will find that your eye is becoming trained to the many nuances of American architectural styles. In the process, not only will your own house renovation be better informed, but you will gain a greater appreciation for the history in houses all around you.

Some Styles of American Architecture

Colonial (1600-1700)
Box-like
Steeply pitched ridge roof with gable on the side
Small windows, symmetrically placed
Prominent chimneys, sometimes central
Upper story may overhang lower story

Federal (1780-1820)
Classical proportions and symmetrical arrangements
Light, delicate, geometric, attenuated decoration
Low-pitched roof, sometimes with balustrade
Smooth facade
Sidelights and an elliptical fanlight over entranceway

Greek Revival (1820-1860)
Adaptation of Greek temple form
Portico supported by classical columns across front
Low-pitched roof
Smooth surfaces, usually painted white

Gothic Revival (1830-1860)
Steeply pitched roofs with wall dormers
Gingerbread trim along eaves and gables
Vertical board-and-batten or stone siding
Pointed arches and hood moldings over doors and windows
Other Gothic features such as oriel and bay windows, pinnacles, turrets, polygonal chimney pots

Italian Villa (1830-1880)
Asymmetrical arrangement of building parts
Smooth surfaces, such as brick or stucco
Low-pitched roofs, either gable or hipped
Wide, overhanging eaves supported by brackets
Windows usually round headed and grouped in twos or threes
Verandas or loggias
Tall, square, corner tower, called a *campanile*

Second Empire (1860-1890)
Symmetrical, square block
High mansard roof with decorative shingles and dormers
Arched and pedimented windows and doors
First floor windows often tall and paired
Chimneys important decorative features

Stick Style (1860-1890)
Tall proportions
High, steep roofs
Widely projecting eaves supported by brackets
Decorative "stickwork" consisting of vertical, horizontal, and diagonal boards, suggesting the structural frame over horizontal siding
Oversized corner posts and roof rafters
Extensive porches or verandas

Eastlake (1870-1890)
Similar to Stick Style, but ornament more three-dimensional
Curved brackets
Decorations such as knobs and spindles reminiscent of furniture

Queen Anne (1880-1900)
Asymmetrical massing, exuberant design
Varied colors and textures, for example, combining brick and shingle or half-timbering in a single building
Upper stories often project over lower story
Windows may contain both small and large panes, and stained glass
Bay windows, gables, turrets, high chimneys, pavilions, porches

Shingle (1880-1900)
Hipped, gambrel, or gable roof, moderately pitched
Convex dormers
Siding of unpainted shingles, sometimes covering even the porch posts
Ground-story walls may be of random rubble or fieldstone
Windows often contain many small panes; may be grouped in pairs or triples
Round turrets and bays

5
CREATIVE WAYS WITH INTERIORS

New Spaces for Old Houses

Sometimes your lifestyle and family size will demand an addition to your old house. Although you might make do with existing space by subdividing rooms or by adapting them to unconventional uses, you often risk spoiling the house by those shortcuts. If you are going to live in this house longer than a year or two, you will want to have your space needs satisfied.

In my own home, for example, I needed a very large room (500 square feet) for meetings and entertainment. I might have removed a nonbearing wall and destroyed two antique fireplaces to gain the space I needed. In exchange, I would have lost the unique functions of two beautiful, symmetrical rooms—a parlor and a guest room—and destroyed two of the four rooms of the original nineteenth-century house. The better solution seemed to be to remove a somewhat awkward, recent porch and to replace it with a 35-foot room across the entire back of the existing structure and extending out to one side. A floor-to-ceiling, arched window, made from a secondhand sash from a house of comparable age, was added on the front of the addition where it extends out from the house. The porch of the addition reproduces the gingerbread found on the front porch of the existing house. In fact, the whole addition consciously preserves the style of the original house, with the exception of a double-insulated glass wall across the whole back, which is admittedly contemporary for the sake of modern materials and convenience. This compromise is somewhat modified by rustic trim, varnished floors of reused, random-width hard pine, and a collection of antique glass on a shelf between the lower and upper windows of this glass wall. I was also able to install a woodstove, which does not barbarize my old house and yet adds some degree of heat to the whole house. Although in some cases one can tastefully add a woodstove to the central hall, mine did not lend itself to that. Since the new addition sits a third of a story lower than the main house, heat rises from it into the central hall and contributes to heating the entire house.

This solution to my space problem had several advantages: First, I got the kind of space I really needed. Second, I was able to avoid destroying existing spaces in my old house, which I valued for both their appearance and unique functions. Third, I got rid of an obtrusive addition to the house, replacing it with one that looks planned rather than like something that happened by chance. Fourth, I gained an efficient source of additional heat for the whole house.

Additions

An addition is a sensible way to make more space of exactly the kind you need. A *shed-roof addition* added to one wall of your house is the cheapest and most common. It has the disadvantage of blocking off windows in the room against which it is added. Furthermore, unless skillfully done it can look like a cheap add-on.

A *free-standing* square or rectangular addition, joined by a connecting hallway, is a somewhat less common and more expensive technique. It has decided advantages: It can duplicate the style, roof pitch, and general profile of the main house, is less intrusive on the original house, and leaves the original house windows still usable. Further, it becomes a quite private area in the house.

Tips on Additions
- Avoid additions on or near the front of the house.
- Always match the original style of the house as closely as possible.
- Always try out your projected design on paper before sawing through the wall of your existing house.

Innovations in New Additions

A new addition is the place to try out some of the amenities you have rightly avoided while working on the rest of the house, for fear that you would ruin the ambience and architectural integrity of the structure. Additions are the perfect place to try whatever your architectural fantasy craves:

- Super-bathroom with all the gadgets
- Solar-heated rooms
- Special-use rooms for hobbies or recreation
- Woodstoves
- Out-sized fireplace

Here, too, is the place to use the most up-to-date building technology. After putting up with certain inconveniences for the sake of the charm of an old house, in your brand-new addition you will enjoy

- A separate electrical system with plenty of outlets and fixtures that will not put additional burden on the main system
- A separate heating system that will be efficient and cheap to operate
- A well-insulated, energy-efficient addition that makes up for heat loss in the main building and offers a retreat for uncomfortable days

Attic Space

Additions are not the only way to add space to your house. Another option you can consider is to develop your attic. An attic bedroom or study can be a charming hideaway, and with modern insulating materials it can be comfortable in both summer and winter. Skylights are a helpful innovation to make attic expansion more attractive, for they bring lighting into such a setting without the resort to the much more considerable expense of building several dormers. You can choose between skylights that open to let in fresh air and the less expensive, easy-to-install, double-walled, plastic bubble skylights.

Do not install plastic skylights beneath a tree: The sap and debris from the tree will eventually ruin the transparency of the plastic.

Dormers

Dormers do add some additional floor space that skylights, of course, do not. While a dormer may seem an ambitious project, if you plan it carefully, build it light in weight, and finish it quickly, you will be all right. Study dormers on other houses and in books, and choose a style as well as a size and proportions that are appropriate to your house, because a dormer conspicuously adds to, or detracts from, the beauty of the house. There are three main types:

Shed-roof dormer	Roof slopes in the same direction as, but at a flatter pitch than, the main roof; often used on houses after World War I
Flat-roof dormer	Like a shed-roof dormer, but with only enough slope to allow the water to run off; roofed with double-lap roll roofing, with no nails left exposed and seams sealed with cement alone
Gable and hip-roof dormer	Reproduce the roofs on the main house; much harder to build but often considerably more attractive than the shed- or flat-roof types

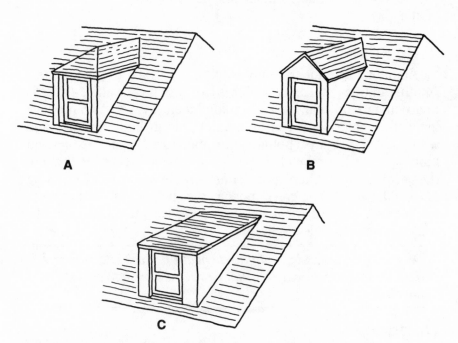

(A) Hip-roof dormer. (B) Gable-roof dormer. (C) Shed-roof dormer.

Stairways Up to Your New Attic Space

New attic space will necessitate a stairway, and planning a stairway requires some mathematical calculations. If space is unlimited, use the ideal proportions for a stairway, which specify 7-inch risers and 11-inch treads, includ- ing a 3/4-inch nosing (overhang). Use the following for- mulas to calcu- late all of your measurements before you begin.

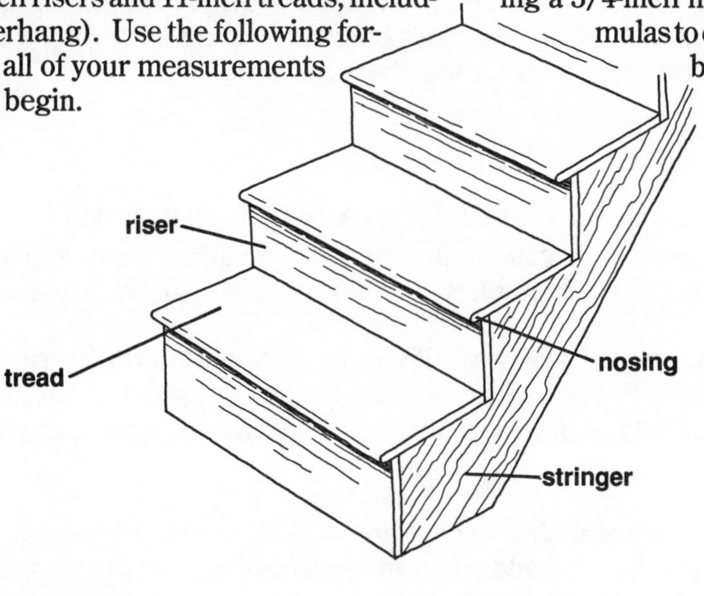

riser

tread

nosing

stringer

Parts of a stairway.

1. To figure the number of risers, take the distance between floors minus the thickness of one stair tread and divide by 7
2. To figure the height of each riser, take the distance between floors and divide by the number of risers
3. To figure the ideal width of a tread (excluding nosing), subtract the height of one riser from 17 1/4 inches
4. To figure the length of the completed stairway, take the number of risers minus 1 and multiply by the widths of the treads (excluding nosing)

It is important to make these calculations accurately, so that the top or bottom step is not of different height than the others. Steps of uneven height are frightening to climb and lethal to descend.

If space is very tight, your stairway will be quite steep with high risers and treads cut to a minimum. Cut the nosing down to 1/2 inch or nothing at all, or you'll never be able to descend the stairs without a safety rope! A narrow tread with an overhang will make you miss the next step as you descend, and you'll go down the stairs as if you were a human toboggan.

Make sure there is enough headroom for a tall person where the stairwell is cut into the upper floor. It would be better to have very steep stairs than to have people whack their heads every time they use your stairs. You could have the distinction of people cursing you for the next eighty years if you don't get this right. If you are unsure where the stairs are going to come out, do not frame in the stairwell until after the stairs are built.

When There is No Room for a Stairway

If space is so constrained that the resulting steep stairway presents an unacceptable safety hazard, there are other options:

U- or L-shaped stairway. If you are making steps that turn, you will need either a landing or wide, pie-shaped steps on the turn, which should be at least as wide in the middle of each tread as the straight steps are.

Circular steel stairs. These are frightfully expensive (unfortunately), extremely handsome, and freestanding (so you don't need walls to hold them up). They are usually put in a square opening.

Custom-made, circular wooden stairs. Supported from a middle pole by hardwood arms going out like the arms of a towel rack, these stairs, too, if made by a cabinetmaker, will be quite expensive. (But see my method of building circular stairs, described below.)

Prefabricated, pull-down, ladder-type staircases. Pull-down stairs are relatively inexpensive and easy to install. You must ascend and descend them facing the stairs.

Building a Stairway

In the past, carpenters went to great lengths to make creak-free stairs. They first routed out the stringers (side members) to contain the ends of the steps and risers, then drove a wedge dipped in glue under each side of the step, into the space they had routed out. Stairs in this tradition are a veritable art form.

Most amateur carpenters today choose to screw cleats to the wall where each step will go and then nail the tread to the cleat. It is very important to screw the cleats, with thin, 1 3/4- or 2-inch screws, into something solid (not just plaster lath) at front and back. Most staircases take a lot of stamping and the cleats will come loose if they are not very secure.

Although this cleat method is a very easy way to build stairs, a better, and more orthodox way is to use precut stringers under each side of the steps. This is fairly easy to do for straight staircases but when you get into U- or L-shaped staircases with pie-shaped steps all the way up, or even just on the turns, the cleat method saves you a lot of complicated calculations: You simply screw cleats to the walls as needed, working from bottom to top.

The Lazy Way to Make a Circular Staircase

1. Figure the riser dimensions as explained on pages 117-18.

2. Plot out an L- or U-shaped area for the stairs.

3. Frame in the walls and ceiling hole.

4. Line the walls with cheap plywood (not particle board: it won't hold screws well enough).

5. Cover walls with wallboard: You will save hours and hours

of work fitting around all those steps and nosings later if you install wallboard before the stairs are put in.

6. Calculate the staircase sections so that there are the same number of steps in each section of the L or U.

7. Mark the stair treads on the outside wall and temporarily nail in the cleats, using 4d nails to facilitate adjustment, if necessary.

8. Mark and place cleats on the inside wall in the same manner. If you are building such a tight staircase that you have a 6x6 (or, less desirable, even a 4x4) post around which the stairs pivot, instead of cleats, cut 3/4-inch boards long enough to span the distance from one step to another. Both the step and the cleat should be the same width as the center post.

9. Cut the treads. They should be at least 1 inch thick or, if possible, 1 1/2 inches. If they are thin, they should be knot-free. If your *circular* stairs have no risers, the tread should be of 1 1/2-inch, knot-free lumber. It is sometimes difficult to figure out the angles of pie-shaped steps; cut cardboard patterns to help get the fit just right. Be sure to make the treads 10 or 11 inches wide in the *middle* of the tread, not the outside.

10. Fit the riser from the back side and screw it into the back of the lower step so that it will support the upper step.

Beefing Up the Ceiling to Support the Room Upstairs

The ceiling joists for the room below your attic addition may need reinforcement in order to serve as the floor joists for your new room. Often it is impossible to add a second joist as large as the original because either the plaster ceiling below interferes or the doubler would stick up higher than the original joist. In such cases, you will have to add to *each* side of the original joist a doubler that is 1 or 2 inches smaller than the original joist (2x6 for 2x8 joists or 2x4 for 2x6 joists). Even better (and cheaper) is a 5/8-inch piece of plywood sawed into lengthwise strips and nailed on each side of the joist. Because the plywood is only 8 feet long, make 60°-angle cuts where the reinforcers must be pieced, and make sure these joints do not occur opposite to each other on the joist. Be sure to nail the doublers to the joist well.

Balconies

Balconies, or lofts, are another way of gaining space if your old house has high ceilings. Although they are not an authentic eighteenth- or nineteenth-century design idea, they add a very nice touch to an old room, especially if you use trim and other ornamentation that suits the style of your house. They can provide extra floor space, access unused space, and add interest to an otherwise plain room.

Use them for
- Guest beds
- Sewing area
- Study area
- Storage

Basement Rooms

Another possibility is to plan a living space in your basement, especially if one or more walls of your basement is mostly above-ground.

The most fundamental task is to assure that the basement is, and will stay, dry. Normally, this involves three precautions:
1. Eliminating groundwater as much as possible
2. Preventing ground moisture from entering the room
3. Providing for overflow in time of heavy rains or flood

Keeping Things Dry
- Lay polyethylene sheeting before pouring cement floors and behind all masonry walls. If walls already exist, consider covering existing walls with polyethylene sheeting and then applying a new wood wallcovering on top.
- Lay plastic drainage tiles under all floors and at the base of all walls. They should be connected with a gravity drain to the outside or to a sump hole, lower than the floor, with a sump pump installed. Be sure to make the whole system slope downhill to the outside or sump hole so that the water won't settle someplace in the drain. A flue tile, filled at the bottom

with gravel, makes a good sump. The gravel will allow water under the floor to percolate up through and into the sump. Add a sump even if you already have a concrete floor and in hopes that it will drain the whole area even without drain tiles.

- Insulate all outside walls with rigid foam insulation behind the wall surface.
- Work on outside drainage to keep groundwater from running into the basement.
- Purchase a dehumidifier for the room.

Keeping Things Warm

Concrete floors that do not have good foundations on the edges (such as a garage floor where there was once a door to the outside) will be very cold, as the heat will be conducted right out through the floor. Place a layer of rigid foam insulation (and a sheet of polyethylene to keep out moisture as well as cold) on the existing floor and add a new floor surface to alleviate this problem. If your new floor is wood, use treated lumber to avoid possible rot from damp conditions.

If the room has a rough floor, you might lay bricks on it, either set in a bed of mortar or laid in a bed of sand. Sweep a mixture of 1 part cement and 3 parts sand into their joints.

For floors in fairly good condition, simply glue down wall-to-wall carpet.

Digging Out Basements

In digging out the basement, it is quite important to work carefully around posts and supporting walls. If a house is set on piers (stout, vertical, structural supports, often made of bricks laid chimney-style), one pier alone may very well carry the weight of two or three automobiles, and thus, even when the earth is barely disturbed, that pier could settle 1/16 or 1/8 inch.

The *minimum* size of the "island" of unexcavated dirt has to be governed by the firmness of the soil. Light, sandy soil is less stable than clay soil. If you have any doubts, leave a large island at first, then cautiously reduce the size of it on one side and install a temporary jack post. Repeat the process on the other side.

Replacing Original Posts

1. Make sure that the concrete will be at least 6 inches deep for an area about 1 foot square just to each side of the post to be removed.

2. Pour the concrete floor and let it harden completely.

3. Put a jack post on each side of the post to be removed. Tighten up the jack post by any means. If you use a jack stop, tighten only until the original post loosens. If you actually pick up the house, you may crack plaster or cause other damage. If you are using wedges, select smooth cedar shingle (not hand-split shingle, which has an uneven surface).

4. Remove the original post. Dig out the dirt on which it rested within the area of newly poured cement to a depth of 2 inches. Fill in the hole with concrete.

5. Cut a treated 6x6, two 4x4s, or a 4-inch steel pipe to the desired length.

6. Drive smooth cedar shingle wedges (shims) above the top of the post *very* tightly. Remove the jack posts.

Although you hope your house hasn't settled at all, it is not the end of the world if the settling is only slight. One way you will know if it's not level is if the doors and windows don't shut properly. A small amount of settling is insignificant and has probably occurred before without you even noticing it. If you feel the problem should be corrected, however, rent a house jack and jack the joist back up about 1/8 inch higher than its final desired level. This allows room for about that much settling on your wedges.

Basements and Their Problems

In many old houses drying out the basement or crawl space can be a major undertaking. Basements have their share of other problems, too, including frozen pipes, various pests, such as termites, and radon gas.

Protecting Your Basement Against the Cold

Depending on the severity of your winters, you may need to give attention to freeze-proofing your basement. In the list below, the very first measure should be sufficient in southern climates, but the further north you live, the more of the list applies.

- See that all air vents close tightly.
- Find and seal all leaks in the foundation with mortar, caulking, and stuffed-in insulation.
- Avoid under-floor insulation, if possible: House heat that filters down can help keep the basement above freezing.
- Glaze any loose windows the basement may have.
- Install a small space heater to use during particularly frigid weather.
- Use rigid foam sheathing to insulate outside walls near pipes. I do not recommend insulating the pipes themselves, because should an insulated pipe become frozen, it will take forever and a day to thaw out, unless you use the new thermally-activated heat tapes, which can be used inside insulation on individual pipes.

Moisture Problems

Wet basements are bad for the house and unpleasant for the people who live in the house.

Install a drainage system inside the basement. Often the water in the soil around the house will force itself down under the basement and up around the edges of the floor. See page 125 for suggestions for laying drain tile and/or installing a sump pump.

Avoid letting water settle along the base of foundations or posts or it will eventually undermine them. Repair by pointing or plastering where past water problems may have damaged the foundation or posts. If bricks in a foundation pier are severely deteriorated, build a form and pour concrete around the offending portion (which usually will be at the bottom where there is the greatest moisture).

Groundwater control is essential. It is not sufficient to deal with water in the basement merely by providing drains and a sump pump or even by having runoff drains where the lay of the ground makes this possible. You must *stop* water from running into your basement if at all possible: It is bad for your foundations, and the basement will remain damp even if it is channeled and controlled by a drainage system. Get serious, therefore, about controlling the groundwater running into your basement. There are at least three approaches to your problem:

- First, redirect the water, before it runs into the basement, by changing the water runoff to keep it away from the house. This can be accomplished by adding gutters to the roof and by installing drain lines for downspouts.
- Better still, pour concrete slabs along the foundations and extending 2 to 3 feet out from the foundations, tapering away from the building.
- Best of all, install exterior foundation drains. The material cost of these is relatively low, and far less than concrete slabs, but the labor is considerable. Make it easier on yourself by doing just one side of the house at a time. Here's how it's done:

1. Dig the ditch at least 3 feet wide, with the surface sloping toward the low side of your property where the drains will carry off the water. Be careful not to dig so far as to undermine the foundation of part or all of the wall: for houses with basements about 1 foot should be fine. Make sure the bottom of the ditch slopes away from the house at least 1/4 inch to the foot, with no dips or hills in it. You want a steady slope so water will not stand in the drains.

sill

foundation

soil

weed-control fabric

gravel

slotted drainpipe

plastic sheeting

An exterior foundation drain can be created by digging a 3-foot wide ditch next to the house, laying in polyethylene sheeting and slotted plastic drainpipe, and filling with coarse gravel covered with weed-control fabric.

2. Lay down a continuous sheet of heavy polyethylene, tacking one side of it to the foundation at a point higher than the original ground level.

3. Install slotted plastic drainpipe along the edge of the foundation. It comes in 10- and 50-foot sections with elbows, Ts, and connectors to make installation easy.

4. Attach an unslotted drainpipe to the lowest end of the foundation drain and route it 4 feet or more away from the house to a location where ground slope will carry the water away from the house.

5. Cover the slotted pipe with coarse gravel, then cover the gravel with a soil separator such as a weed-control fabric that will let water through but keep soil from washing into the gravel and plugging it. Replace the dirt. Try to slope the ground away from the house.

Pests and Plagues in Your Basement

Termites are not merely a basement problem, of course. If you don't do something about them, they will be a whole-house problem. They get their start in the basement or crawl space, however, since they originate in the ground and move up to feast on your delicious house.

Some Words of Wisdom and Caution About Termites

There are three things that termites really like in a home:
• The dark of your basement
• The moisture of your basement
• Much decaying wood that touches the ground

Termite damage is not necessarily a sign that your house is a lost cause, but termites must be stopped before they do damage the whole house irremediably.

Treatment does not mean tearing into the walls and searching for termites. It is enough to cut them off at their supply lines. Consequently, treatment consists in flowing a long-term, residual pesticide around the edges of everything that connects the house with the dirt. Because the pesticides used for this treatment are quite powerful, treatment is most often done by professionals. (Chlordane, which was the time-honored chemical for killing termites, was found to be a carcinogen and has been banned.) The technique used involves digging trenches along the foundations and posts, which then are flooded with the solution. Hollow masonry walls are drilled and the liquid is pumped in. If you have a well near the house, however, insect control professionals will not perform this treatment for fear of a contamination suit.

Reconstruction After Termites

Hopefully, the doubling of termite-damaged joists or wall studs will be adequate repair. Use pressure-treated lumber to avoid future problems with either termites or rot. In areas devastated by termites, however, it is best to tear out and rebuild. In the long run, you will probably save labor and materials by so doing.

The Newest Scourge: Radon Gas

This is the latest scare for all houseowners, not just owners of old houses. It is not the kind of problem that is a threat to you today or tomorrow, but one that you would not want to live with over a number of years. You can test your basement with readily available, relatively low-cost kits. It is best to test your house in the winter, when the basement area and the house itself are not ventilated and the readings are thus highest.

The geological characteristics of your area are the most important factors determining whether or not you have a radon gas problem. Rock or shale seems to allow the gas to migrate more readily than it does in areas with damp clay. Other contributing factors are
- Lack of ventilation in the basement or crawl space
- Lack of ventilation in the house itself (actually less likely in old houses than in new)

Various authorities recommend different methods of treatment for radon gas problems. The following advice is commonly accepted:
- Seal all cracks in masonry-walled and concrete-floored basements with caulk—usually a tough problem in old houses. Seal the traps in all floor drains, then use a small fan in the area to put a slight pressure on the drains. This keeps all drain areas flushed with fresh air and keeps gas from building up in them.
- Ventilate the basement to the outside.
- Eliminate all holes where air could get up into the main struc-

ture of the house from the dirt area.
- If possible, use polyethylene to cover the dirt in an unfinished basement or crawl space or the underside of the floor.
- After treatment, use another test kit to monitor improvement.

Interior Renovation

The revival of the inside of your house may well be 50 percent of the task. It is certainly the part that changes the structure from an antique *house* to an antique *home* and gives you great rewards for your work every day of your life. Although as with the outside work, you will want to be sensitive to the original design of the house, you will need bathrooms, a modern kitchen, a modern electrical system, and a modern form of heat. This is why I have called my approach "reviving" rather than "restoring" an old house. This antique must be comfortable and suited to your needs for particular kinds of space. Not only is your home your castle, as in old English law, but your castle—this nice old house you've been working on—is your *home*.

Commonsense goals are to preserve
- The flavor of antiquity in all things
- The look of antiquity in most things
- The basic creaturely comforts that one expects in a home
- A minimum of trouble and maintenance
- Reasonable operating costs

Walls and Ceilings

The walls of your house will probably need some form of attention, and you will need to consider what level of attention they need.

Possible Problems of Old Walls	
Problem	Solution
Cracked and nicked plaster	Patch small holes with joint compound and larger holes with patching plaster. Tape large cracks with joint tape just as you tape new wallboard (see pages 133-34).

Problem	Solution
Very old paint that continues to chip off and powder	Scrape off all that you can, and cover with a coat of oil-based paint. Finish-coat with latex wall paint.
Bumps and gouges in the plaster	Break off the loose and protruding plaster, and patch with joint tape and joint compound.
Large quantities of moisture on walls	Check the outside of house for severe moisture problem, such as siding that needs painting and gutters that soak walls. Install ridge or gable vents and eave vents.
Loose plaster pulled away from the lath	Try screwing it to the lath behind it with self-tapping screws; plaster over screw holes and cracks. If this does not work, remove loose plaster and insert wallboard patches on top of the lath. Tape to the surrounding plaster with wallboard tape. Rough up the smooth surface of the wallboard with a brush and joint compound to imitate the surrounding plaster, or with a steel trowel if the adjacent surface is very smooth.

Patching Plaster Walls and Ceilings

Plastering is one of those things that looks harder than it is, but it takes practice. There are three secrets to successful plastering of cracks and holes in plaster walls:

• *Use the right materials.* The stuff they call patching plaster is usually ridiculously high priced. You would do better to go to a building-supply dealer and buy an 80-pound bag of plaster and use this for the rough coat in all patching jobs. You should be aware that sometimes what is called patching plaster is really plaster of paris, which you may have used as a child to make little wall plaques. If you need to fill a deep hole, it is excellent, but it sets up very fast, so mix only what you need. Joint compound makes an economical and good material for the final coat over patching plaster or for covering small blemishes in the existing plaster. (Don't use joint compound to fill the large holes themselves, because it shrinks a lot when it dries.)

- *Clean the area* to be plastered of any old, loose plaster.
- When applying regular plaster over lath, *wet the lath down* just before plastering with a generous spray of water from a plastic spray bottle with the nozzle set to mist.

Re-covering Walls with Gypsum Wallboard

Sometimes the walls are so bad that you need to replace them with a new surface. The first step is to prep the walls:

- Remove all loose plaster, including everything that is not tight to the lath.
- Fill all resulting holes with lath or shingle to bring the area to be patched up to the original level of plaster.
- In some cases, such as where large areas are loose or where the surface is very uneven, you will have to remove all the plaster.

Before putting up the wallboard is the time to install any new electrical lines and outlets that are needed. Be sure to mark the location of the wire on the surface of the wallboard so that you don't hit a wire when nailing in the wallboard.

This is also a good opportunity to add insulation to outside walls. If you have removed plaster, take down the lath, too, and insulate between the studs (see pages 74-75). If you are leaving the old plaster in place, add 1-inch, high-density rigid foam insulation over the old plaster before installing your new wallboard. If the increased wall thickness protrudes beyond your window and door casings, you will have to build them out.

For best results, use a cordless screwdriver and long, self-tapping screws (popularly called Sheetrock screws). Self-tapping screws have sharp points and deep grooves in their Phillips head slots so that they can be driven with a cordless screwdriver. They are called self-tapping because they will pierce even soft tin without a starter hole. They have several advantages over nails:

- Since they don't have to be driven into studs, you don't have to place your wallboard joints over studs.
- You don't have to pound them in, so you don't risk loosening plaster on nearby walls.
- Screws don't work loose, as nails do, with expansion and con-

traction of framing.
- You can drive screws into lath that would be too springy to get a nail into.
- Self-tapping screws will hold in sheetmetal.

Cover the joint where new wall and existing plaster meet with joint compound and tape (see pages 133-34).

How to Build Out Door and Window Casings

When you cover an existing wall with wallboard, especially if you also add insulation, you may have to build out door and window casings because the surface of the new wall lies beyond the casings. There are two methods for doing this:
- The purist's method involves removing the casings and the apron (the flat, horizontal member under the windowsill), being very careful to not split the wood. Next build out the jambs (the uprights that form the side of the opening) to the level of the new wall with wood strips of appropriate thickness. Replace casings. If you are planning to remove the paint from the woodwork, you might consider sending the casings to a professional paint stripper. You should also put new sash cords or chains on the weights while you have them exposed.
- An easier method, if the window and door casings do not already have a trim molding, is to add a molding around the outsides of the present casings. Ordinary "colonial" window casing material is usually suitable. If that does not build the casing out far enough, add a strip of wood under the molding to bring the trim out to the necessary level. On the other hand, if windows and

---

Removing old trim may not turn out to be as easy as you think it will be. It is often brittle with age and held in tightly with many layers of paint. Proceed with caution and patience to avoid splitting and splintering.

---

doors already have moldings, you will have to try a different approach. If the outside edge is flat, you can build it out as far as 3/4 inch by nailing on a strip of wood the same width as the outside edge. If the situation requires building it out more than 3/4 inch, you would do well to remove the moldings, add pieces of wood to bring the casing out to the necessary level, and then

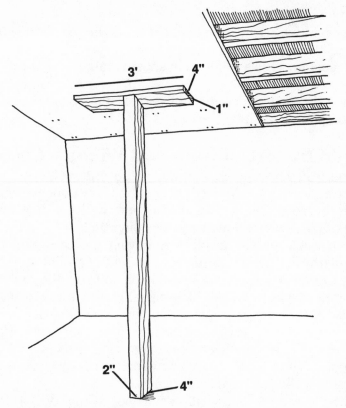

Use a wooden brace to hold wallboard in place until you can nail or screw it permanently to the ceiling joists.

replace the original moldings. Baseboards may also need to be removed and then replaced on top of the wallboard.

New Wallboard for Old Ceilings

In the case of ceilings, as in the case of humans, just hanging around for fifty or seventy-five years is hard on the ability to hold together. Ceilings thus usually deteriorate before walls do, and badly deteriorated ceilings should be covered with wallboard. Never try to lift loose plaster with a layer of new wallboard. You will have to remove the loose plaster before applying your new ceiling. For small problem areas, remove loose plaster, shim the area where you have removed the plaster to bring it to level, as you do on walls (page 130), and cover the entire ceiling with wallboard.

To apply wallboard to ceilings, construct two big Ts, the horizontal members of which are 3-foot long 1x4s and the vertical members of which are 2x4s about 1 inch longer than the ceiling height. Put the wallboard in place, at the same time forcing these Ts up against the wallboard to keep it in position until you get it nailed or screwed permanently to the ceiling. Screw the ceiling into the lath and, wherever you can, into the joists. A cordless screwdriver is especially useful for this job.

Simple Lessons on Taping Wallboard

Everyone has his or her own method of taping wallboard, but I'll share with you my own experience. Use ready-mixed joint compound sold in five-gallon cans. What a service to humanity it was when this premixed variety became available so that it is no longer necessary to start from a powder as we did in the old days. Make sure you don't get any old pieces of plaster or dry joint compound into your supply of fresh joint compound or it will leave furrows in the surfaces you are trying to smooth.

1. Cut a piece of tape the correct length and set it aside. Apply a first coat of joint compound in which to embed the tape. With a broad taping knife (a very wide wallscraper may also be used), spread a coating of compound down the whole length of the joint. Downward pressure will keep gaps from developing in the compound. Press the tape into it with the knife. When you get to corners, cut the tape and fold it lengthwise into a long v-shape, as with flat seams, before applying the joint compound. Let this coat dry thoroughly. (You can apply a very thin coat of compound over the tape before this first drying, but it isn't necessary.)

2. Apply a second coat of joint compound to cover the tape. Trying to hurry this and subsequent steps will just give you a bad job and a big headache. If you try to cover the tape completely on the first application, you will surely get the tape so wet that it won't stick and you will have bubbles in the tape or whole sections of it rising up in rebellion.

3. Use a very wide taping knife to apply a third and, better still, additional coats of joint compound. Patience really counts at this point. If you omit this step (as I shamefully admit that I sometimes do) you will be able to spot the joints and nail holes at a thousand feet on a cloudy day. What you are trying to

accomplish is a build up of thin layers of compound over the tape, spreading out from 8 to 10 inches on each side and thus tapering the edges so that no ridge is visible. Generally, I find that smoothing the material perpendicularly with the joint works best, though others prefer working parallel to the joint.

4. Nail heads and damage marks also must be covered with at least three coats of joint compound, the last one going out from 1 to 5 inches all around the nail. Joint cement shrinks somewhat, so each coat will leave a new depression until the final coat is applied.

5. To get absolutely smooth walls, finish the job by sanding the joint compound. This, unhappily, is a really dirty job. After it's dry, you can work out some of the ridges with the help of a wet sponge.

Use these same techniques when you must repair holes in the walls. Apply a chunk of wallboard or patching plaster to the hole before you tape it.

Good luck on this. It is likely that you will do better than you think you will—and you certainly will improve with experience. If you are going to paper the wall or ceiling, you don't need to do quite as careful a job as you need to do where only paint will hide your work. You will soon find out that although wallpaper hides minor flaws, paint hides almost nothing.

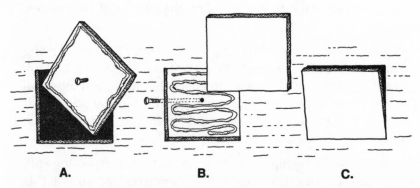

A.   **B.**   **C.**

(A) Using the screw as a handle, put filler patch through hole in existing wallboard and glue the filler patch to the back of existing wallboard. (B) After glue has dried, cut a plug the exact size of the opening, and (C) glue it into place against the filler patch.

Commonsense Wallboard Repairs

When the wall that needs repair is made of wallboard, you will usually need to use a different approach. *Damaged areas* can be cut out to the nearest stud. Nail a piece of scrap lumber—called a *nailer*—to the stud so that you have something to which to attach the patch. Headers can be nailed or screwed at the top and bottom of the hole so that half of the width supports the old material and half supports the new at the point of the horizontal joint.

Patching a Small Hole in Wallboard

1. Make the hole rectangular or square.

2. Cut a filler patch, to which the final patch will be fastened. This should be a piece of wallboard or lightweight wood bigger than the hole, but of such a size that it will fit through the hole diagonally.

3. Put a screw in the center of the patch to use as a handle.

4. Apply white glue to the front surface of the patch, around the edges only.

5. Slide the patch into the hole; you may have to do a little cutting to get it in.

6. Use the screw handle to pull the patch toward you tight up against the back of the existing wallboard until the glue dries. If it is very heavy, you might need four screws through the old wallboard to hold it.

7. Cut the final patch, a plug that fits the hole exactly.

8. Cover the patch with glue and insert the plug into the hole against the filler patch, fastening it in with joint tape and joint compound.

Wallpaper and Painted Walls

Amazing improvements in the quality and the variety of wall coverings have recently become available. The choice is yours, but those choices present some challenges. Here are some suggestions from my own hard-won experience:

• Do not spend all of your nickels on wallpaper—less interesting houses need this kind of pick up, but not your beautiful old house.

• Do not choose wallpaper that is inappropriate for an old house.

- Do not choose colors and patterns that are too striking and bold. Today's wall coverings last for decades, so avoid what you will soon tire of or will find hard to mix with new furniture or the changing uses of rooms.

Advantages of Wallpaper over Paint

- Wallpaper, especially vinyl wall covering, which is very tough, will help hold the plaster together.

- Wallpaper seems actually to prolong the life of the plaster by keeping it airtight.

- Wallpaper is great for covering walls with small cracks and slightly rough surfaces.

- Wallpaper, especially vinyl or vinyl-coated wall covering, will usually provide a vapor barrier.

- Wallpaper will outlast several paint jobs. Although, like paint, it fades, paint also begins to flake off in a few years and it probably shows dirt more than patterned wallpaper does.

Tips for Hanging Wallpaper

Before hanging wallpaper, remove layers of old wallpaper and apply a sealer to the wall. If the wall surface has been painted, always use a *latex sealer* so that any stain in the plaster can't come through. The sealer also helps to keep the paint under the paper intact, otherwise the paper may curl up at the joints where the old paint stuck to the paper and the paint pulled off the wall. When this happens, nothing will get it to stick to the wall again.

I like to use *vinyl paste*, even for prepasted paper, because I think it sticks better, and there is more time before the paste dries to adjust the paper while working. Be careful, however; if you apply too much paste to prepasted vinyl wall covering, bubbles that won't go down will form beneath the surface.

If you decide not to use paste on the prepasted paper, do not just wet it with a brush, but soak it in water according to the manufacturer's instructions. If wallpaper does later come loose, glue pieces back up again with wallpaper paste.

- The easiest method of fitting wallpaper is to cut it several inches longer than necessary and then to trim it along the baseboards and ceiling edge with a sharp, single-edged razor blade after it is hung securely in place.

- The best way to fit wallpaper around windows, doors, and other interruptions is to cut it larger than necessary, then to trim it with a single-edged razor blade as you are attaching the sheet of paper to the wall. In the case of a door or window opening, for example, rough out the hole a little smaller in size than the actual opening, *before* you spread the paste on the wallpaper. If you are putting up prepasted paper, make your cuts before you get the paper wet. Smaller openings, such as those for switches and electrical outlets, can be cut out once the paper is on the wall.
- Gently but firmly smooth paper out with a wallpaper brush. (Some delicate papers may show brush marks, so proceed cautiously.) Roll down the joints with a hard roller to make them stick well, and make sure there are no bubbles under the joints that would leave a piece of the paper not glued.

Don't be intimidated by wallpapering. It is not as difficult as it used to be when papers were more fragile than the tough ones on the market today.

Papering Ceilings

Although not impossible, ceilings are admittedly hard to do. Avoid them if you can. With papered walls, painted ceilings look better anyway! If you feel you must paper the ceiling, here are some tips to help you along.

- Set up a good scaffold, such as a heavy plank between two stepladders.
- Cut the paper a bit longer than necessary before applying paste.
- Fold back one 18-inch section with paste against paste. Then, fold the rest crossways, accordion fashion, into a number of 18-inch sections with *right* sides always against right sides and pasted sides against pasted sides.
- To apply paper to the ceiling, unfold section by section, working your way across the ceiling and smoothing the paper as you go.

Tips on Paints and Painting Interiors

- As with exterior paint, for interiors I recommend using high-quality, though not necessarily the very best-quality, paint available. If you can, get good, name-brand paint at sale prices.

- Re-cap paints tightly. You can save even the smallest amounts and combine them when you get a substantial amount to get some free paint. Never mix oil and latex paints, but you can mix indoor and outdoor paints, gloss and flat, as long as paints are all latex or all oil.

- Save money by painting your rooms all the same color. Because in fine old houses it is not the wall color that is the center of beauty, you can get away with this better than you can in less interesting houses.

- Spread heavy drop cloths everywhere so you won't spend half your allotted time in clean up.

- Use a telescoping roller extension for both ceilings and walls.

- Don't overpaint walls and ceilings; thick layers of paint will inevitably crack and peel.

Wood Trim: Strip It or Paint It?

If your house is older than 1920, its woodwork was probably originally stained and varnished. With the passage of time, these varnishes often darken so much that they appear to be black paint. By all means strip off this old stuff. Varnished wood strips relatively easily. In fact, that original coat of varnish often is a real lifesaver, for, in many cases, it will have prevented subsequent paint layers from filling up the pores of the wood. Try one door frame at least, and if it is too much work, you can always paint over your half-hearted attempt at stripping. Paint that has been applied over varnish also strips fairly well, but paint laid over bare wood is almost impossible to get clean unless it is dipped.

If you really want varnished trim, you can remove all the casings and have them dip-stripped professionally. Unfortunately, you may split many as you try to remove them, and you will still have the jambs and sashes to do. A more sensible compromise is to remove and strip the doors, preferably by having them dipped. If you strip them yourself, lay them in a horizontal position where you can get serious about putting lots of paint stripper on them. The trim can then be painted in contrasting colors to show off its ornateness. Varnish the doors while they are still off the hinges and without hardware.

Unfortunately, when the old-timers were staining what they considered an inferior wood with a coarse grain, such as yellow pine or fir, they often applied a ground coat of a paint-like substance to obscure the grain. It is the worst part of the accumulated layers of finish to get off, and when you go to varnish it, it will look bleached and chalky. In this situation, radically thin the first coat of new varnish with the recommended thinner for that particular type of varnish. A 50-percent mixture would not be too thin. If you even suspect problems, put a test coat on the edge of a door and let it dry to see what the whole job is going to look like.

Paint that has been applied over a good primer on bare wood is very hard to get clean enough to stain or varnish unless it is dipped in a tank. It is well-nigh impossible to get rid of the little flecks of white paint in the surface. If you try to stain over them, the stain will just go into the bare wood, leaving the white spots to show up even more conspicuously than before. In this case, try a stain-varnish which, instead of permeating the wood as stains usually do, acts more like a paint, covering up the surface.

Generally, you should not stain old doors or other old wood. The very fact of its age means that it will turn surprisingly darker as soon as any kind of varnish is applied to its surface. If the door is a recent reproduction, however, test a spot on the edge of the door. If it shows that it is not going to match the other doors when it is merely varnished, experiment with stains until you find one that matches. Do the same for other replacement wood, such as casings and flooring.

As you strip away old paint and varnish, you may find that some old deceiver in past years used a piece of plywood or putty or plastic wood to patch something up. You may find a mantel with plaster trim, a door with an added width or length made out of some nonmatching wood, or some other unexpected disaster. Try covering these with flat brown paint, then applying stain and wiping it off with a cloth or a brush to simulate wood grain.

Tips on How to Strip Paint and Varnish
- Get lots of cotton cloth: T-shirts and other cotton knits are especially good. You may be able to find a place that sells rags cheaply by the pound.
- Protect your skin, and especially your eyes. Most strippers are exceedingly toxic.
- Work with your surfaces horizontal so you can lay a lot of stripper on the wood. This is no place to be delicate.
- Use good-quality stripper and buy it by the gallon. Use the

gel form for both horizontal and vertical surfaces, the liquid form for horizontal surfaces only.

- Liquid stripper can be applied using a plastic, pump-type garden sprayer. Small items can be dipped in a panful of stripper; reclaim your stripper by straining it through a screen to clean it.

- Let the stripper do the work. Wait until it blisters the paint before you try to lift off the paint.

- Use a broad scraping knife, such as a putty knife. First get the large part of the paint off of the flat surfaces, then use cloths to wipe as much of the surface dry as you can.

- Apply multiple coats of stripper. You won't succeed in getting all the layers off in one try.

- When the wood is clean, flush it with water, but avoid soaking the wood any more than you have to.

Floors

The treatment of the floors of your house will be determined largely by the condition that time and misuse have left them in.

Special Floor Problems

Problem	Solution
Painted or dark, varnished floors	Sand and refinish them, using very heavy paper on the sander, until all the color is gone.
Badly marked floors	Sand floor, starting with medium paper.
Warped floors	Wet them and try to screw them down while they are wet. If you can get the floor fairly level, it may be sandable; otherwise, you will need to replace particularly offending boards and then carpet the room.
Badly creaking floors	Shim up the joists from underneath. It is said that sweeping talcum powder into the joints helps.
Floors that look good but lack a finish	Wet-mop them using a strong cleaner. Allow them to dry thoroughly and revarnish.

Common Floor Finishes

Finish	Characteristics
Floor varnish	Fairly outmoded because it gets brittle with old age and shows scratches
Polyurethane	A clear plastic finish, which, unless laid over bare wood, may peel. Apply the second coat within twenty-four hours, or, if more than twenty-four hours elapses, sand the first coat before adding the second coat. It is tough and waterproof, but it cannot be waxed. High gloss is tougher: satin finish has had a sand combined with the polyurethane.
Shellac	A time-honored floor finish that is rarely used anymore except to coat over existing shellac. It covers most other finishes, gives an excellent finish for waxing, and can be touched up or second coated. It is not waterproof, however, and turns white when it gets wet.
Wax, or wax over linseed oil	An old-fashioned finish that is unsatisfactory in the presence of bett alternatives, because it requires constant attention for minimum good looks. If any finish other than more wax is added over it, the original wax must first be completely removed with a wax remover.

Floor Sanding

This dirty and tedious job gives great rewards in a short time. You will get better at sanding with practice. The job will certainly be easier if you follow this advice:

- Consider taking up warped or uneven boards and placing shims under them to level them before sanding. Sometimes the shimming can be done from the basement so that you don't have to tear up the floors.
- Rent good-quality equipment from a reliable company.
- Floor-sanding machines require a 20-amp circuit, with nothing

else running on the circuit.

- Because it is such a filthy job, try to do all your floors at the same time. Also, for the same reason, refinish your floors before painting walls and trim.

- A high-powered exhaust fan in the window of the room being sanded will cut down dramatically on dust in the house.

- Hang wet sheets over openings into other parts of the house to keep the dust from travelling through.

- Use the correct paper: *Coarse paper* is for leveling and for taking the old finish off; sand with it until you see all bare wood. *Medium paper* is for smoothing the floor somewhat and removing the abrasions caused by the coarse paper. *Fine paper* is the final touch to get the floor so that it feels smooth to your hand.

- Sand *with* the grain of the wood. Some people pull the machine, but you can sand in both directions as long as you always move the sander with the grain.

- The most important thing is to keep the sander touching the floor gently while *constantly* moving it forward or backward. Every time it is allowed to drop on the floor abruptly, or to remain in one place, it will leave a trench the same width as the sanding drum, which will show in the finished floor. Don't get bent out of shape when you get a few of these trenches—all amateurs do. They are not nearly as visible in a furnished room as they are in a bare room with a new coat of varnish on it!

- Switches on the handles of some sanders allow you to raise the sander so it is running on the drum and not the wheels once the sanding drum has contacted the floor. Slowly go the length of the floor, tapering off to nothing at the very end. Alternatively, you can sand to the middle of the room from both ends and carefully taper the sanded strokes on the second end to meet the stopping place for the first end.

- As you sand, watch for the shiny nail heads and drive them in with a nail set as soon as they appear. Otherwise, they will groove the sandpaper and probably make it fly off the drum.

- Do the edges with the special edger that is always rented with the sander.

- Corners where the edger cannot reach may be scraped clean with a *sharp*, broad chisel. Hold the chisel, or a good triangular scraper, perpendicular to the floor surface with both hands and scrape toward yourself, at the same time exerting downward pressure.

- Clean up the sawdust with a shop vacuum or broom, followed by a dust mop dampened with linseed oil if you plan to varnish, or by a commercial tack rag if you will use polyurethane.

- Roll on a coat of varnish with a paint roller and extension handle (so you don't have to bend over or work on your knees). You don't even have to use the roller pan. Just pour out a small amount of varnish on the floor and roll it in.

Hardware

The hardware in your old house will probably need attention. Among other possible problems, it may have eight or ten coats of paint on it.
- Don't paint it with gold paint and try to make people think it is brass: They won't think it's brass; they'll think it's tacky.
- If it is speckled with white paint, paint it black.
- If it has many layers of paint on it, remove it and dip it in a bucket of paint remover to clean it thoroughly.
- If it is just rusty, cover it with shellac and then highlight the

---

Any old brass that your house may contain can be cleaned with steel wool and brass cleaners. Once it is thoroughly clean, spray it with a clear lacquer to keep it from dulling again. This will keep you from coming to hate the frequent cleanings so much that you end up painting it. By the way, I have known instances where silver-plated hardware was covered with wall paint and beautiful, solid brass painted with gold leaf. Watch for unexpected blessings beneath all the paint! When in doubt about whether a piece of hardware is brass or not, use a magnet to test it.

---

edges and any embossed high spots with a rub-on paint similar to shoe polish, made for this purpose. Apply it with your finger and then, when it has dried a bit, buff it with a soft cloth. The result looks like a million dollars! It not only shows up any embossing or engraving, but gives the effect of old brass shining through years of grime.

- Avoid spending too much on what I call "designer hardware," reproduced to sell to perfectionists with old houses, especially if you have demands more central to the beauty, comfort, and efficiency of your old house than minute but costly details.

Lighting Fixtures and Chandeliers

Brass or painted tin lighting fixtures that need to be restored should be taken down and examined.

- Use steel wool and brass polish on the solid brass, and household cleanser on brass plate. Spray freshly cleaned brass with several coats of clear lacquer.
- Repaint painted surfaces as needed.

Interior Doors

Nothing in an old house lends so much to the general ambience of antiquity as do beautiful doors. If you are fortunate enough to have all the doors you need right there in all the correct openings or stored away in the basement or attic, count yourself lucky. This isn't always true, however, and you may have to be inventive to work out some compromise if you are missing a door or two. My first advice is never to put a plywood flush door in an old house. A more acceptable choice is *masonite doors*. Molded to look like old doors, they look, feel, and sound new. They are usually six-panel doors, however, not the usual four panels that many old houses have. A molded door may get you by until you run across a nice old door that will fit your opening at a garage sale some day. If the rest of your doors are finished natural, you might try antiquing the molded door so that it doesn't stand out like a sore thumb.

- In the case of missing sets of *pocket doors* (large, sliding doors typically used in late nineteenth-century houses between such rooms as hall and parlor or parlor and dining room and fashioned so as to slide into the walls), you might try building an ornamental lintel across the top of the opening supported by two or four columns going all the way to the floor or to a half wall. Leave ample space for passage between these projecting dividers.

- If your talents run to design, you might try designing and making your own doors. Molding and cut-outs with ball-and-

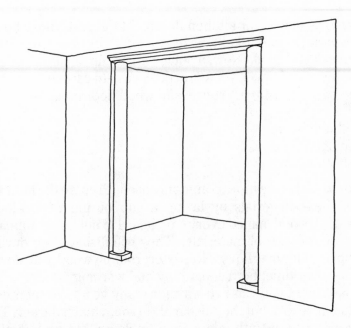

If pocket doors are missing, build an ornamental lintel across the opening and install columns against the vertical frames.

dowel decorations can be applied to plywood doors and then painted. Be sure your design suits the style of your house.

One of the loveliest doors I have seen is a true primitive design from a cabin up in the mountains. Made of three vertical tongue-and-groove boards, it has three horizontal panels with rounded edges nailed onto the finish side of the door. A similar one could be made out of pine for less than the cost of a cheap plywood flush door.

Kitchens and Bathrooms

Kitchens and bathrooms often claim major attention when homes are refurbished. In addition to planning ways for these rooms to function more efficiently for your family, you will want to give thought to their flooring and cabinetry. Your kitchen may have nothing more than a sink and a bare minimum of cupboards—if any cupboards at all. Often, freestanding china cabinets and Hoosier cupboards (which featured flour sifters and pull-out, porcelain work counters) served all the household's needs.

Wood floors are now a distinct possibility for kitchens or bathrooms. This is quite in keeping with the old custom of using a white wood, such as maple, for kitchen floors. In the past, these floors were not varnished, but kept clean and white by constant scrubbing with salt and sand. Now, a polyurethane finish allows one to have the beauty of wood, yet a practical, easy-to-care-for finish as well (see pages 140-43). A successful wood floor must be

- Tight
- Smooth surfaced
- Undamaged

Tile or *linoleum* are more commonly used. Prepare the floor for either of these materials by laying a subflooring of 1/4-inch, waterproof plywood, nailed every 6 inches. Do not use chipboard or other nonwaterproof materials: They will disintegrate during the first plumbing overflow. Nonwaterproof plywood will slowly deteriorate over time, both separating and warping.

Choose colors you can live with for many years. Remember, dark colors hide dirt, but they also make a room much darker. Tile is much easier to fit to the floor than linoleum, but high-quality linoleum makes a more waterproof surface, and tile often warps and loosens along its many seams. Consider ceramic tile for bathrooms. Although it is about twice as expensive as good vinyl tile and requires the same plywood underlayer, it lasts for the life of the house.

You have several choices of what to do about *kitchen cupboards*. You could take the option of freestanding cupboards, but this will almost certainly leave you with an outmoded sink, no place to put a dishwasher, and too little countertop workspace. Furthermore, a lot of little cupboards and cabinets are apt to look very cluttered. The other extreme is to have a factory-built, modern kitchen installed, leaving this one room in the house a startling contrast to antiquity.

The middle way is to install a limited number of cabinets and countertops and a modern sink. With this option, you can create the desired ambience with such antiques as a freestanding primitive cabinet, a Hoosier cupboard, a pie safe, or iron bakers' racks. Use an antique or reproduction butcher block in the center of the room for a work island and additional countertop working space. Hang your cookware and utensils over the stove area, to cut down on the need for cupboard space. Careful consideration of the lighting system for an old kitchen will help enormously in creating the right atmosphere, while, at the same time, give a sufficient amount of light for a modern kitchen.

Prefabricated cupboards represent a huge investment in something that does not go well with an old house in the first place. Two alternatives will both save you money and look better.

- Buy just the doors and make your own cupboards.
- Make the cupboards in their entirety, with perhaps the exception of laminated plastic countertops, purchased in ready-made lengths, which you can then cut to fit.

How to Build Cupboards (or Bookshelves) the Pinch-penny, Lazy Way

- Mark out the position for the shelves on the wall.
- Screw wood strips (1x12s or 1x2s) to the wall just below the shelf marks, using slender, self-tapping screws and a cordless screwdriver. To keep the whole cupboard from pulling off the wall, it is especially important to screw the strip that will support the upper shelf into the studs at various points.
- Nail or screw shelves to the strips.
- Add ends, where necessary, by nailing through the end pieces into each shelf. Be sure the shelf is level before nailing in place. Shelves will tend to slope toward the front because of their own weight if not level. If the end of a shelf is against a wall, screw a short strip to the wall to support its end.
- Build door casings on the front of the shelves. To determine the size opening you need, evenly divide the space, ascertain what size doors are available, and keep doors fairly narrow both so that they do not project hazardously when open and so that the weight on the joints is not excessive.
- Construct doors of vertical boards held together with 1x1, horizontal strips screwed at the end of the boards, top and bottom. This is an old method that gives a sturdy door, a finished look, and the appearance of age. Alternatively, you could build narrow frames, screwed together at the corners and routed out to be fitted with glass. Or plywood doors can be made exactly the size of the hole minus the width of a dime all the way around. Plywood doors done in a commercial shop ordinarily overlap, but they are hard to build without the right tools.

Fireplaces

Everybody loves a fireplace, but they do demand some close

attention to make them efficient and safe to use (for some advice about chimneys, see pages 103-5). The first task is to eliminate the draft going out through the chimney. It will suck the heat right out of your house, whether you have a fire going or not. There are two ways to do this:

- Assuming that the chimney is in perfect condition, you might use the fireplace for occasional fires and build an airtight cover to plug into the fireplace opening when it is not in use. A box-cover design, about 4 inches or so deep, will work better than a flat piece of wood or tin. If you come across an old metal fireplace cover (used at one time to block off fireplace openings permanently), attach it to a plywood box structure; it will make a good plug and the plywood will keep it from falling over.
- Another option is to install an airtight fireplace insert, which works like a woodstove. This will be possible only if your fireplace is deep enough. In the Southeast where I live, most houses have shallow fireplaces, good only for burning coal.

Other Fireplace Wisdom

- Often the elaborate mantels and mirrors of the late nineteenth-century are merely screwed to the wall and can be easily removed for stripping and refinishing.
- Fireplace tile can be replaced, if necessary, with ordinary ceramic tile.
- If you are doing a radical job of interior restoration, you might choose to tear out the chimney and build a new, flue-tiled one. If you work from the top, you can avoid destroying the opening and firebox of the existing fireplace.

Electrical System

There are two ways to deal with the fact that your house does not have a big enough electrical system. The first is to have it rewired. Generally, if you have heavier lines brought in from the pole, an electrical inspector will require that you have a qualified electrician rewire your house. If you plan to do this, the earlier you do it in your renovation process, the better, and the cheaper.

The second option for dealing with an inadequate electrical system is to make do with the present service by expanding the lines and by radically curtailing your use of electricity. If you have a system that has at least half a dozen circuits (indicated by the number of fuses there are in the fuse box), and if you do not depend on electricity for cooking, heating, and hot water, you might get along with the present service.

You might also try some conversions and avoid complete rewiring. Systems that have a circuit (or sometimes even a separate meter) installed for a hot water heater and/or an electric range have the potential for expansion. Since the electric stove is 220 volts, and the hot water heater probably is also, if both stove and heater were converted to gas there would be four extra circuits that could be used for circuits elsewhere in the house. As you add extra lines to existing circuits, think ahead and balance them so only one large appliance, such as the refrigerator, freezer, toaster, dishwasher, attic fan, is on each circuit.

Your old house may have a knob-and-tube electrical system. There is nothing wrong with such a system if

- You are using electricity for lighting only (*no* appliances), in which case a ground is unnecessary
- There are no frayed or loose wires
- Nothing is near the lines that could fray them or short them out
- The receptacle outlets on the walls, the switches, and the ceiling fixtures are all in good condition. This means that switches feel tight, plugs fit snugly in receptacles, and ceiling fixtures have no frayed wires.

Plumbing

Plumbing has gone through a revolution in just a few years, making it now a do-it-yourselfer's delight. Materials are relatively inexpensive compared to those used until recently, and further, they are easy to cut and install. For example, you can use plastic soil pipe that glues together, and flexible neoprene connectors that join new plastic to old cast-iron pipes.

You can choose between two different systems for water pipe:
- *Flexible, polybutylene pipe* with pressure-tightened joints is about the same price as copper and easy to cut (can be done with a knife) and assemble. Because it is flexible, it is somewhat freeze-proof and it is tough.
- *P.V.C. and C.P.V.C.* (Polyvinyl chloride and commercial polyvinyl chloride) is the white- or cream-colored material that is most commonly used. It is cheap, easy to use, effective, safe (no lead problem here), and rust-free, and it can be cut with a hacksaw and glued together. However, it can be broken, and it will

shatter if frozen with water pressure on. It is important to use C.P.V.C., the more expensive of the two, for at least the hot water lines.

Sewer Lines and How They Work

If you do not have your own septic system, your private sewer line most likely connects with the public sewer line in the middle of the street in the front of your house. Drain systems have a gentle slope, or pitch, toward the sewer in every horizontal part. Before the advent of plastic pipe, terra cotta was used. Roots often get in through the joints in the pipe and clog the line. If that happens, call a drain service or rent a rooting-out machine.

Every drain from the house into the drain system must have a trap, which consists of a U-shaped pipe that is always filled with water to keep odors and gasses from coming back up the system into the house. Near each trap is a vent pipe going up higher than the eaves of the house to allow gasses to escape into the air.

Plumbing Repair

If you have to get involved in plumbing repairs on either water or sewer lines, it may be better to repair than to replace the whole line with new materials, depending on the general condition of the line and the location of the problem. Here are some common problems you may face:

Leaking Sewer Pipe

- First, clean the section to be repaired well, and allow it to dry; use a hair drier to speed this process along. For a temporary repair, wrap the leaky pipe tightly with electrician's tape or duct tape.
- For a permanent repair, replace the offending section with plastic pipe with neoprene coupling clamped onto the old pipe. You should be able to get the old section out by melting the lead in the joints with a butane torch. Alternatively, old sewer pipe can usually be broken by driving successive holes around it with a sharp metal punch. Any jagged ends can be broken off by adjusting a crescent wrench to the thickness of the pipe wall and snapping the jagged piece off.
- If the leak is in the joint of cast-iron sewer pipe, dry it out and try sealing it with silicone sealer.

Leaks around a Toilet Base

- Turn off water supply.
- Drain the tank.
- Unfasten the water inlet line.
- Remove the two to four bolts holding the toilet to the floor.
- If the floor is rotted out, cut out a square section of floor to the nearest joists and replace it with a new waterproof plywood section of floor with a hole cut for the sewer pipe.
- Install a new wax seal on top of the sewer pipe, being certain the seal is on right side up.
- Carefully replace the toilet.
- Fasten and reconnect the water line.

Leaking Sink Traps

- First, try tightening the offending joint, while holding the rest of the trap firm.
- If that does not stop the leak, and the trap still looks in good shape, try adding new washers.
- If that does not work, remove the whole assembly and replace with a P.V.C. trap. Use silicone sealer generously where the new plastic system meets the old drain.

The adaptors that allow you to go from galvanized to plastic are the worst aspect of plastic piping and need to be screwed on to the metal with the help of teflon tape or some other sealer. Buy a couple of extra adaptors so you can risk breaking them by screwing them on very tight. They won't leak when you turn the water back on.

Leaking Galvanized Pipes

- First, turn off the water supply and remove the whole section, from one threaded joint to the next. You can then replace this section with two pieces of pipe and a union, which allows you to screw together pipes coming from two directions, or, you can add adaptors at each pipe joint and insert a piece of plastic pipe in the middle.
- If the leak happens to be a pinhole leak (as is often the case in an underground water line), it can be repaired temporarily by

clamping a plastic patch against the leak. One pinhole leak, however, usually signals corrosion to the point that it will probably spring more leaks soon.

Leaking Copper Pipes

- Remove the leaking section with a tubing cutter or (carefully) with a hacksaw. Use polybutylene fittings for your repairs because polybutylene is the same size as copper pipe and readily accepts the relatively soft copper.
- If there is just one break, perhaps because the pipe was frozen, a polybutylene connector section will nicely fit around the leak. For multiple leaks, put a connector section of polybutylene on each end and a length of polybutylene pipe between them.

6

LANDSCAPING FOR THE OLD HOUSE

Tastes in landscaping vary widely. Some homeowners strive for a well-kept football field, others wish to create an Amazon jungle. Whatever your preference, however, some general principles should be considered:

- Deciduous trees are particular assets for nonair-conditioned houses, cooling it in summer and, when trees are bare in winter, allowing it to drink sunlight in through the windows.
- Plan landscaping to enhance, not hide, the special features of your beautiful old home.
- Use shrubbery to hide any unattractive features.
- If for cost considerations choices must be made between house repair and shrubbery, house repair should usually take precedence.
- Minimize the number of plants that need constant tending, such as hedges that need frequent clipping, roses, and tender shrubs that don't overwinter well in your area.
- Plant shrubs and trees well away from wood or stucco houses to minimize rain splash against the house.
- When you plant foundation shrubs, remember how much bigger they are going to be when they mature, and put the root ball at least 4 feet away from the building.
- Trim tree branches that hang too close to the house, especially if they touch the roof or wall in the wind or rain.

Walks

If you have no walkways around your property, your may wish to create some. Make some observations of current and desirable traffic patterns before you begin. Once you have decided where walks are needed, consider what materials would be most suitable.

- Use natural materials such as flagstones and brick, laid without mortar, in places where the definite lines of a concrete walk would be intrusive.
- Raise your walk several inches above ground level so that it doesn't become a river bed every time it rains.
- Increase the thickness of concrete walks that cross driveways so that they won't break under the weight of vehicles.
- Always use a form to contain the poured concrete, or it will break away where the edges are thin.

Concrete Walks

Poured-concrete walks are safe, long-lasting, easy to keep clean of debris and snow, and fairly simple to install. When purchasing concrete, plan on 1 yard of concrete for every 80 square feet of surface.

Tips on Choosing Concrete	
Type	Use
Bagged concrete mix (in 80-pound bags)	For small projects, such as setting a mailbox or a gate post
Gravel, sand, and portland cement	For medium-size projects, such as footings for two or three posts in the basement; transport it yourself from gravel company in trash cans
Ready-mix concrete	For larger projects, such as walks; check to see if you can share a load with a neighbor—there is often a surcharge on less than 4 or 5 yards

Preparing Wooden Forms for the Concrete

- Make forms out of 1x4s or 2x4s, using cost-free or leftover materials, if possible.
- Place the forms on edge along the line of the walk, and stake

Build a sturdy concrete form before laying cement and use a 2x4 to screed, or level the concrete to the tops of the forms with a sawing motion.

them with pegs driven into the ground outside of the forms at intervals frequent enough to hold them firmly in place. The forms are sometimes nailed to the stakes to preserve the right height and prevent the forms from collapsing inward.

- Cut stakes off level with the top of the forms before pouring the concrete so that they won't be in the way when you level it.
- Make curves out of plywood, staked frequently to force them to keep their shape.

Laying the Concrete

- In a wheelbarrow, mix concrete, using 3 parts gravel, 2 parts sand, and 1 part portland cement. Strive for as stiff a consistency as will still allow you to pour: The stiffer the concrete when it is poured, the stronger the finished product. If you run short, you can fill the area with stone or brick and then cover this completely with concrete.
- Using as a leveler a 2x4 that is a few inches wider than the form, level the concrete to the tops of the forms with a sawing motion. This is called *screeding*.
- Places where the vertical edge of the concrete will show after the form is removed (such as a step) require special treatment. Hammer on the face of the form with a big hammer to bring liquid to the surface and free it of any air pockets.

- When concrete is beginning to dry, but still wet enough to show a finger mark, smooth it with a rectangular trowel.
- For a mirror finish, trowel it a second time when it is almost dry, but soft enough to show a mark from a nail or stick.
- Leave the forms in place for two days to cure the concrete thoroughly. Otherwise, corners and edges may break when forms are removed.

Leftover concrete could be a disposal problem: Always prepare a location for extra before you begin the project.

Always wear gloves when handling concrete and mortar. You will have blisters all over your hands if you don't.

Brick Lawn and Garden Walks

You may be lucky enough to become heir to various bits and pieces of brick of different sizes, which can be made into an unobtrusive walk across a lawn. *To lay an informal brick walk,*

- Cut a path of the desired width through the sod. (Use the good sod that you remove to patch bare spaces in the lawn. Prepare the bare spot by turning over the earth to loosen it, press the sod firmly in place, and water it well.)
- Lay bricks in either a regular or irregular pattern on the top of the soil. Use whole bricks along the outside edges for stability. Leave 1/2- to 1 1/2-inch spaces between bricks.
- Shovel soil over the bricks, and sweep it into the cracks, leaving surface of bricks clean.
- Sow grass seed over the bricks, and sweep seeds into the cracks.
- Spray with a garden hose set on mist.
- When it dries, you may need to sweep another layer of fine dirt over the walk to fill cracks completely.
- Nurture as you would any new-sown grass, being particularly careful to keep it well watered, and mow cautiously until grass becomes sod and holds the bricks firmly in place.

For a more formal walk, lay bricks on a bed of sand, using a level to even the surface as you go. Leave 1/8- to 1/4-inch spaces between the bricks, then sweep a 50-percent mixture of sand and portland cement into the cracks. Finish by sprinkling gently with a garden hose set on mist.

Alternative Walks

Walks can also be made out of flagstones, gravel framed by 2x4s, or wooden walks made of treated 1x4s, 2x4s, or 2x6s laid on 2x4s. Railroad ties make sturdy walks, laid in either lengthwise or, in short sections, crosswise. (Ties are a mess to cut, however, and the creosote in them may ruin your chain saw.)

Driveways

Avoid the expedient of paving everything with a hard surface such as asphalt or concrete. Such a driveway may look neat and clean as you contemplate the idea, but in reality

- It is likely to kill some or all nearby trees by starving the roots of water.
- It is unnecessarily expensive.
- If you use asphalt, you will have to give it considerable maintenance.
- It may cause or compound drainage problems.

A far better, mud-free driveway is one of gravel or crushed stone. It is cheap and ecologically responsible, and can be improved or even removed at a later date, should you wish.

EPILOGUE

And now, dear reader, having spoken in many words about the subject that is of so much interest to us both, I commend you to your task of renovation with all its pain and toil and difficulty, but with its equal amounts of fulfillment, growth, learning, and immense satisfaction. Do your work well, keep your eye on the day of relative completion (though you will never *really* be finished); enjoy the fruits of your labor as you go along. Above all, do not get discouraged. Even the smallest amounts of progress will eventually bring you to a measure of completion.

I'm sure that the day will come when you will look back on your experiences as a house renovator as some of the most rewarding of your own and your family's life. You will have learned well the lessons of thrift, patience, and discipline, and will appreciate the enhanced value of something you have labored for and put a part of your very life into. I will imagine you someday sitting in the rich environment of an elegant parlor surrounded by your own handiwork and bathed in the aura of five or six generations who have previously called this home. In such a setting you will deservedly reflect on the great privilege accorded to those who live in a well and thoughtfully cared for antique.

I urge you to share your home generously with visitors and strangers, encourage others to treat the artifacts of earlier generations in the gentle, loving way you have done, and lend a helping hand and a word of useful advice to others who have undertaken the task of renovation.

Glossary

Adjustable-rate mortgage. A loan in which the interest rate wanders up and down according to the current inflation rate

Amperage. The strength of an electrical current, measured in amperes

Apron. The flat, horizontal member of a window, under the sill

Baluster. An upright support for a rail in a balustrade

Balustrade. A row of balusters topped by a rail

Beam. A long timber used as one of the primary horizontal, supporting members of a building

Bracket. An overhanging member projecting from the wall to support a vertical load or to strengthen an angle; also used for decorative effect

Capital. The topmost part of a column

Casing. The enclosing frame around a door or window opening

Caulk. A waterproof, soft, pliable material used to seal joints and cracks against water or air leakage

Circuit breaker. Similar to a fuse, but unlike a fuse, contains a switch so that it can re-establish the flow of electricity instead of burning out. See also Fuse

Cornice. The top, horizontal, usually projecting member of a wall

Crawl space. In houses without basements, the area beneath the house between the floor and the ground, usually at least 24 inches high

Damper. A movable plate in a chimney, which when opened permits smoke and fumes to be drawn through the flue to the outside, but which when closed reduces the rush of cold air into the house

Dormer. Upright, roofed projection on a sloping roof, usually containing a window

Downspout. A vertical pipe, usually connected to the gutter, which carries rain down from a roof

Eave. The lower portion of the roof that overhangs the wall

Fascia. A horizontal piece covering the joint between the top of a wall and the eaves

Fixed-rate mortgage. A loan in which the interest rate and thus the monthly payment remain the same over the time of the mortgage

Flashing. A sheet metal used to waterproof roof valleys or the angle between a vertical wall, such as a chimney, rising out of a roof

Flue. Passage in the chimney through which smoke and fumes from the fireplace travel

Foundation. Supporting member of the wall, constructed usually of concrete, brick, stone, or concrete block

Fuse. A disposable contact consisting of a thin wire element; used in an electric service panel to permit electricity to flow through, but to burn out and deactivate if the circuit is overloaded. See also Circuit breaker

Gable. The triangle formed by the sloping lines of the roof from the eaves to the ridge

Gambrel roof. A roof with two slopes of different pitches on each side of the ridge

Gingerbread. Pierced, curved decoration fashioned by a jigsaw or scroll saw, often used under the eaves of roofs, both on the main house and on porches

Glazing compound. A pliant material used to hold a pane of glass in a window sash

Gutter. A trough, either built into or attached to the eaves to catch and carry off rainwater

Hipped roof. A roof with slopes on all four sides

Jamb. Upright member that forms the side of a door or window opening

Joint compound. A premixed, plaster-like material used for patching holes in plaster walls and covering seams and nail holes when installing wallboard

Joist. Small horizontal timbers laid parallel from wall to wall to support a floor or ceiling

Latex paint. A synthetic rubber- or plastic- and water-based paint

Mansard roof. A roof with two slopes on all four sides, the lower slope being much steeper than the upper

Molding. A projecting, decorative strip

Nosing. The rounded front (and sometimes side) edge of a stair tread that projects over the riser

Pier. Stout, vertical, structural support, often made of bricks laid chimney-style

Pitch. The degree of slope of the roof. Pitch is measured in inches rise per foot of run. For example, a 45-degree roof has a 12-inch rise.

Plasterboard. See Wallboard

Plinth. The lowest part, or base

Pocket doors. Large, sliding doors typically used in late nineteenth-century houses between such rooms as hall and parlor or parlor and dining room, and fashioned so as to slide into the wall

Post. A vertical supporting member of a building

Primer. A base coat that prepares the surface for the finish coat of paint

Putty. A pliant material consisting of hydrated lime and water

PVC. Polyvinyl chloride; white- or cream-colored plastic plumbing pipe; CPVC is the commercial, more expensive, and better-quality type

Rafter. One of a series of parallel beams that establish and support the pitch of the roof from ridge to wall

Railing. A horizontal member of a balustrade

Remodel. Modernize and improve an existing structure with little regard for its original character. See also Renovate; Restore

Renovate. Modernize and improve an existing structure while at the same time maintaining as much of its original character as possible. See also Restore; Remodel

Restore. An attempt to return a building to its exact condition at some point in the past, even if it means losing many modern conveniences. See also Renovate; Remodel

Ridge. The topmost horizontal line where the upper slopes of a roof meet

Riser. The vertical member between two stair treads

Roll roofing. A roofing material made of asphalt-soaked felt with a gravel surface, available in a long sheet, usually 1 yard wide and 36 feet long

Rubble. Unshaped stones used to form an irregular wall surface

Sash weight. Part of the mechanism of double-hung windows, which supports the weight of the sash and maintains it at a desired height; weights usually hang over pulleys on the end of sash cords or sash chain

Sash. The part of the window framing that holds the glass; sometimes refers to the entire movable part of the window

Self-tapping screws. Phillips screws with sharp points and deep grooves in their Phillips head slots so that they can be driven with a cordless screwdriver. They are called self-tapping because they will pierce even soft tin without a starter hole

Sheetrock®. See Wallboard

Shim. A thin, often tapered piece of wood used to fill a space to level

Siding. The outside skin of a frame building

Sill. A horizontal timber that is usually the lowest supporting member of a building; the lowest supporting member of a window casing

Soffit. The area of the roof that extends over the walls of the house; also referred to as the overhang or the eaves

Soil pipe. A pipe for carrying off waste water from the toilet

Stool. A finish piece of molding installed on top of the windowsill and extending beyond the window casing

Stringer. A horizontal, supporting member

Stud. One of the smaller uprights in the frame of a building, to which sheathing, paneling, or lath is applied

Subfloor. The wooden base that is attached to floor joists in preparation for finish flooring

Sump pump. A water-removal pump located in the basement

Tread. The upper, horizontal portion of a step

Tuck-point. Process of partially removing old mortar from masonry joints, cleaning the joints, and applying new mortar to them

Valley. A diagonal trough formed where two sections of the roof join at right angles

Wallboard. A board used as a substitute for plaster, consisting of a hardened gypsum plaster core bonded to a fiberboard or paper protective covering. Also known as plasterboard, or by the tradename Sheetrock

INDEX

F

Federal architecture, 111
Fiberglass insulation, 73-78
Fireplace,
    inspection of, 27
    restoration of, 147-48
Flange maker, **56**
Flashing, **32, 101**
Floors,
    inspection of, 25-27
    restoration of, 140-43
Folding ruler, **48**
Foundation, **117**
Framing square, **49**
"Free" houses, 65-66

G

Gable, **32**
Gardens, walk restoration and repair, 156
Glazing, of windows, 90-93
Glazing point, **91**
Gooseneck wrecking bar, **50**
Gothic Revival architecture, 111
Greek Revival architecture, 111
Gutter, **32**

H

Hacksaw, **56**
Hammer, **48**
    tack hammer, **52**
Handsaw, **48**
Hand sledge, **51**
Hardware, restoration of, 143-44
Hatchet, carpenter's, **51**
Heating system, inspection of, 19-20
Horizontal top panel, **90**
Hot water heater, 17-19, **18**
House inspection,
    ceilings, 22-24
    checklists for, 34-40
    equipment needed, 13-14
    of exterior, 29-34
    floors, 25-27
    heating and hot water system, 17-19
    insulation, 27-28
    interior of house, 19-29
    plumbing and water lines, 16-20
    roof, 28-29, 31-33
    underneath house, 14-15

water and sewer lines, 16-17
wildlife evidence, 28
wiring, 28
House purchase, 5-40
    cost analysis, 6
    inspection process, 12-37
    location as factor, 38
    negotiating price, 9
    owner-sold houses, 9-10
    real estate contracts for, 11-12
    size as factor, 38
House renovation,
    of attics, 114-18
    of chimneys, 103-5
    of doors, 93-97
    efficiency ratings of insulation, 75-76
    insulation methods, 72-79
    landscaping, 153-58
    of masonry surfaces, 79-82
    moving a house, 69-70
    old-house treasures, 60-63
    organizing for, 41-47
    painting, 80-88
    of porches, 97-103
    of roofs, 105-10
    of storm doors and storm windows, 78-79
    tools for, 47-60
    tuck-pointing, 81-82
    walk restoration and repair, 154-57
    weatherization, 71-79
    of windows, 78-79, 90-93
    of wood exteriors, 82-88

I

Insect pests, detecting during house inspection, 15
Inspection, See House inspection, 12-37
Insulation, **75**
    efficiency ratings of, 75-76
    house renovation and, 72-79
    inspection of, 27-28
Interiors, in house renovation, 128-52
Italian Villa architecture, 111

J

Jack plane, **51**
Jigsaw, **53**
Joint tool, **81**

Joist, **15, 23**

K

Kitchen, inspection of, 20
Kitchens, restoration of, 145-47
Knives,
    broad, **52**
    pocket, **52**
    putty, **52**

L

Landscaping, 153-58
Level, **49**
Lid lifter, **57**
Lighting fixtures, restoration of, 144
Living areas, inspection of, 21
Loans, in house purchase, 7

M

Masonry surfaces,
    house renovation and, 79-82
    inspection of, 29-30
Mason's hawk, **81**
Moisture,
    in basements, 124-26
Mortgages, types of, 7-8
Multiple listings, real estate contracts
    for, 11-12

N

Nail puller (cat's paw), **50**
Nail set, **49**
Needle-nose pliers, **56**
Net listing, definition of, 12
Nosing, **117**

O

Old-house treasures, 60-63
Open listing, definition of, 12
Outdoor equipment, in house renovation,
    55-56

P

Painting,
    exteriors in house renovation, 82-88
    removing old paint, 83-83
    selection of paints, 85-86
    spray painting, 87-88
Pests, in basements, 126-27
Pick, **55**

Pipe cutter, **56**
Pipes, repair of leaking, 150-52
Pipe wrench, **56**
Planes,
    block plane, **51**
    jack plane, **51**
Plastering, 128-31
Pliers, electrician's, **56**
Plinth, **98**
Plumber's tools, in house renovation, 56-
    57
Plumbing systems,
    improvements for, 149-52
    inspection of, 19-20
Pocket knife, **52**
Points, in house purchase, 7
Porches,
    inspection of, 30-31
    ornamentation on, 110-12
    repair of, 97-102
Post, **15**
Posts, repair and replacement of, 102-3
Power tools, in house renovation, 53-60
Pre-used materials, house renovation and,
    64-65
Priming, of exteriors in house renovation,
    84
Property taxes, in house purchase, 8
Pry bar, **50**
Putty knife, **52**

Q

Queen Anne architecture, 112

R

Radial arm saw, **54**
Radon gas, 127-28
Rafter, **23**
Railings, repair and replacement of, 102
Reciprocating saw, **53**
Renovation, See House renovation
Ridge, **23, 32**
Rigid foam sheathing, 73-78
Riser, **117**
Roller, **57**
Roof,
    inspection of, 28-29, 31-33
    raising of, 102
    renovation and repair of, 105-10

"R-value", for insulation, 75-76

S

Sash brush, **57**
Saws, **53-54**, **56**
Screwdriver, **48**
Scriber, **49**
Second Empire architecture, 112
Sewer lines, improvements for, 16-17, 150-52
Sheetrock, 130-35
Shingle Style architecture, 112
Shingles, in roofing, 108-9
Shovel, **55**
Shutters, 88-90
Side rail, **90**
Siding, painting of, 84-85
Sill, **15**, **117**
Sinks, repair of, 151
Sledge, **51**
Sliding T-bevel, **52**
Slotted drainpipe, **117**
Soil, **117**
Space, increasing of in old houses, 113-28
Spray painting, 87-88
Stairways, building of, 117-20
Staple gun, **52**
Sticker, **68**
Stick Style architecture, 112
Stone foundation, **15**
Storm doors, 78-79
Storm windows, 78-79
Stringer, **117**
Stud, **75**

T

Tack hammer, **52**
Tape, **51**
Tape measure, **48**
Taxes, in house purchase, 8
T-bevel, sliding, **52**
Termites, 126-27
Tin snips, **52**
Toilets, repair of, 151
Tools,
   in house renovation, 47-60
   see also specific tools by name
Tread, **117**
Trims, repair and replacement of, 102

Trowel, **81**
Tuck-pointing, 81-82

U

Unheated attic, **76**
Utility knife, **49**

V

Valley, **32**
Ventilation, weatherization and, 77-78
Vise, **51**
Vise grip, **52**

W

Walks, landscaping of, 154-57
Wallboard, **75**, 130-35
Wallpaper, hanging of, 135-38
Walls,
   inspection of, 24
   insulation of, 73
   renovation of, 128-40
Water-sewer lines,
   improvements for, 150-52
   inspection of, 16-17
Weatherization,
   in basements, 124-26
   degrees of gain in, 73
   house renovation and, 71-79
   insulation methods, 72-79
   "R-values" for insulation, 75-76
   storm doors and windows, 78-79
Weed-control fabric, **117**
Wheelbarrow, **55**
Window, sills painting, 84
Windows,
   inspection of, 25
   repair of, 90-93
   storm windows, 78-79
Wire snippers, **56**
Wiring,
   inspection of, 28
   see also Electrical system
Wood exteriors, in house renovation, 82-88, 135-40
Wood trim, restoration of, 138-40
Woodwork, inspection of, 24-25